MW00904393

PRAISE FOR
FAITH-BASED

"Mike Gafa is an administrative leader with experience in business (leadership development), the local church (Executive Pastor), and a regional group of churches (administrative leader). He has written *Faith-Based* in a way that reflects his depth of faith, strength of character, and proficiency in organizational planning. The book is rich with Scriptural passages and principles. It provides a toolbox of resources. Get this book if you are serious about advancing the Kingdom through responsible organizational planning."
Burt Braunius, President of Church Leadership Center, Grand Rapids, MI

"I have known Mike Gafa for over a decade and consider him a friend. We have partnered closely in ministry and I respect him greatly. He brings the unique perspective of one who has been an effective leader in both the marketplace and the local church. If you want to move your church, NPO, or Christian organization forward with crystal clear vision that honors Jesus and is true to Scripture, take time to learn from him. It will be time well spent."
Rev. Kevin G. Harney, Lead Pastor of Shoreline Community Church, Author, and Visionary Leader of Organic Outreach Ministries International (www.kevingharney.com)

"The Church often has to walk a tight line with wisdom and faith, planning and remaining open. Mike Gafa helps ask better questions so that church leaders can walk that line with humble confidence. *Faith-Based* is a Biblically-rooted, theologically sound, practical tool for leaders to pray with passion, plan with discernment and take the next step of faith personally and with their congregations."
Rev. Andrew Bossardet, Coordinator for Equipping Thriving Congregations, Reformed Church in America

"So often a church is driven by fear or data rather than the Spirit and Scripture. In contrast, Mike Gafa's *Faith-Based* helps churches to rely on God's calling, relevant information, and God's purpose for the Church to live more fully into God's mission. In *Faith-Based*, Gafa uses his great love of God and cunning knowledge of business to be a blessing to the Church. I recommend this book to anyone looking to lead a church into God's purpose for their local setting."
Rev. Ryan Landt, Pastor of Aberdeen Reformed Church, Grand Rapids, MI

"When I first got to know Mike, he was a member of the church I served and a leader in the business community. But he had a big and holy discontent going on; God was calling him into church ministry. Mike listened. Our church hired Mike as Executive Director of Ministries. Then, Mike continued his pastoral development by becoming a Commissioned Pastor while he continued to serve the church. In his executive leadership role, we benefited from Mike's wisdom and leadership. God used him tremendously to lead in building ministries with impact and a church planting movement. Use these proven tools and resources. If your heart beats for fruitful and faithful Gospel ministries, as does mine, *Faith-Based* will help unleash your church."
Rev. James Lankheet, Executive Director of Church Leadership Center, Holland, MI

"Mike Gafa is a church leader/consultant whom I hold in high regard because of his calm and faith-filled approach to the life and health of the congregations with whom he works. *Faith-Based* moves us away from fear and fact based planning. I love the idea of trusting God, making plans from the perspective of faith and holding our plans loosely, so that we can adjust as God leads us along the way. Mike's thoughts and tools are helpful in navigating these challenging waters in challenging times for the church of Jesus Christ!"
Rev. Rick Veenstra, Regional Executive of the Great Lakes Region, Reformed Church in America

"It is so good to see *Faith-Based* come together. Having worked with Mike and experienced many of the principles in the book, you will be encouraged in setting a course for your church and ministry. Mike is a leader who loves the church and is able to lead missional change."
Rev. Eric Cook, Lead Pastor of Remembrance Church, Grand Rapids, MI

"Mike Gafa and I have known each other for almost two decades, and my life has been so much richer for our friendship. In *Faith Based,* Mike integrates a clear sense of how strategic planning functions at a benchmark level combined with a thoughtful, biblical perspective. He makes a compelling case for why churches are wise to invest time in thinking deeply about who they are, what they specifically have been called to do, and how to most effectively carry out this calling. Any church large or small would do well to seriously consider this excellent tool to implement the important task of strategic planning."
Jack Zandstra, Executive Director, Lakeshore Habitat for Humanity, Holland, MI

"Mike Gafa does a masterful job in reminding us that regardless of the size of your church, or culture of your church (because you have one), God has called you to lead, and to lead well. I found great freedom in discovering that as a senior pastor, I am not solely responsible for discerning the vision of the church, and that effective leaders glean wisdom from other leaders God has surrounded them with. Mike has created a resource to truly engage our entire team into a process where God's vision for 'our' church can be found."
Rev. Les Wiseman, Lead Pastor of Knapp Reformed Church, Grand Rapids, MI

"I like the way that Mike integrates his business knowledge and planning experience with his understanding of how the Holy Spirit often works at revealing future actions. I can give his process my full support to any that are considering using it."
Rodger Price, Owner of Leading by DESIGN, Zeeland, MI

Faith-Based

A Biblical, Practical Guide to
Strategic Planning in the Church

MICHAEL GAFA

For the pastors and leaders who earnestly and passionately labor for the cause of Christ.

CONTENTS

Part 5

Alignment

Part 6

Execution

Key Tools

MICHAEL GAFA

INTRODUCTION

Faith-Based encapsulates much of what I have learned in ten years of helping to lead churches through a variety of planning processes, and fifteen years of helping to lead teams in the corporate sector. Faith-Based is a comprehensive guide to biblical, practical planning in the church, and serves to assist and equip churches, pastors, and lay leaders to step more fully into the Great Commission given to us by Christ.

I have much to share in the pages that follow, but for now I'll start with three basic thoughts:

First, like myself, there are many church leaders who initially learned how to plan while working in the corporate sector. A word of caution: the knowledge you have picked up is valuable, but be careful how you use it. If we plan in the church the same way we do in corporate America, we will end up with churches that value bottom line results over progressive transformation, magnetic leadership over humble followership, and self-sufficiency over Christ-dependency. In short, we'll end up with churches that resemble corporations.

Second, planning is not only biblical, it's essential. Yet many pastors and leaders avoid planning altogether, believing that since Christ is building His church, planning isn't necessary, and may even be a distraction. This train of thought misses the point that even as our Lord is building His church, He has given us a commission - a co-mission - that binds us together with Christ and one another, and merits that we use everything we have at our disposal.

Third, *how* we approach planning is critical. Our perspective must always be, "Thy will be done." When we hold our plans too tightly, when we start to think we've got everything figured out, we are in deep trouble. You won't find the phrase, "My will be done" anywhere in scripture, and for good reason! But releasing control is difficult because it goes against our inherent desire to be in control.

As it relates to planning, whereas the intent in the marketplace is centered on controlling as much as possible in order to bring about a specific, positive result, in the church the opposite is true. In the church, we are called not to take control but to *release* control, giving our own agendas, our own dreams, our own expectations over to God, asking (and expecting) His will to be done. Is this easy? Not hardly! But it's what we're called to do, and do it we must.

Faith-Based is designed to keep the focus on God while discerning what God is calling us to do. I strongly recommend that you work through the material slowly and collaboratively with leadership and staff teams. Parts one through five typically take around a month each, with part six ongoing throughout the fiscal year.[1] The approach provides ample time for you and your leadership team to absorb and discuss the material, and to work together on the tools provided in *Faith-Based*.

Godspeed and God bless!

PART ONE

PREPARATION

1

FAITH-BASED PLANNING

The mission of every church is to honor the call God has placed on us to make disciples – in our homes, communities, nation, and world. The question before us is, "Have we stepped fully into God's call upon us?" And if we're honest about it, this question is not an easy one to get to "yes" on, at least not if our eyes are open to the enormity of what it means to step *fully* into God's call. So … where do we even begin?

We begin with one step … then another … and another … and still another. But we don't step blindly or haphazardly, lest we wander off course without even realizing it.

Steven Covey taught that we must always begin with the end in mind.[2] But is what Covey advocates biblical? Or more to the point, is planning biblical?

> "The plans of the diligent lead to profit as surely as haste leads to poverty." (Proverbs 21:5)

Planning does in fact have a place in the Christian life, and helps us to avoid making hasty decisions that lead to poverty – to ruin.

"Commit to the Lord whatever you do, and your plans will succeed." (Proverbs 16:3)

It is imperative that we submit our plans unto God. Why?

"Many are the plans in a man's heart, but it is the Lord's purpose that prevails." (Proverbs 19:21)

In summary then, diligent plans lead to gain, but our plans must always be set apart for the Lord and held loosely, because invariably God's purpose prevails. This point is captured beautifully by Henry Blackaby, who wrote that, "God reveals His purposes so you will know what He plans to do. Then you can join Him. His plans and purposes will not be thwarted. They will succeed. The Lord foils the worldly plans of nations, but His plans come to pass. Planning is not wrong. Just be careful not to plan more than God intends for you to. Let God interrupt or redirect your plans anytime He wants to." [3]

THREE APPROACHES TO PLANNING

It seems to me that there are in essence three approaches to planning that churches can take: fear-based, fact-based, and faith-based. And while it is obvious that faith-based organizations ought to make plans that are rooted in faith, the truth is that far too many churches, knowingly or unknowingly, make plans that are rooted in fear or fact, rather than in faith.

Fear-Based Planning

"Fear of man will prove to be a snare, but whoever trusts in the Lord is kept safe." (Proverbs 29:25)

The paradox is this: If we're consumed by fear about what people think about us, or say about us, or even do to us, and we give into fear by capitulation or appeasement, then the path we've chosen is not safe but a snare – a trap. Fear causes paralysis; fear keeps us stuck in place. Fear can drive a person to take his talent and bury it in the ground, and fear can drive a church to either not plan at all, or to make the same plans and budgets time and time again. No matter how much we try to dress up our plans, if we are rooted in fear, the result is always stagnancy.

Fact-Based Planning

"Trust in the Lord with all your heart and lean not on your own understanding." (Proverbs 3:5)

Whereas a fear-based approach to planning leads to spiritual paralysis, a fact-based approach leads to spiritual blindness. We focus so intently on what we can see that over the course of time we lose sight of what we *can't* see.

As an administrator, I am all too familiar with the tendency to make fact-based plans. What we want is data, and lots of it! That way we can formulate data-based plans and data-based budgets and data-based goals and data-based charts ... and become increasingly myopic. But let's establish that data in itself is not the problem; rather, the problem comes when we become more data-driven than Gospel-driven, more reliant on facts than on faith, more trusting of what we can see than what we can't see.

In Numbers 13, God gave Moses a command to send some men to explore the land of Canaan, which was to be given to the Israelites. Forty days later the men returned with their update: *Great news! The land is overflowing with milk and honey, just as God promised! We even brought some fruit back – it's yummy!*

Unfortunately, ten of the men didn't stop there. *There is one little, or uh, big issue though. How shall we put this? The men in Canaan are HUGE! And powerful! And so are their cities! It's like we're grasshoppers in their sight. There's no way we can defeat them. But, hey, at least we brought back some fruit, right?*

Thankfully, two of the twelve – Caleb and Joshua - trusted more in the unseen promises of God than in what they saw with their eyes. And forty years later, they were the only two adults from their generation to enter the promise land.

There will be times when we are surrounded by people who are mired in fear, or blinded by facts. In those moments - and at all times - God calls us to remain faithful, resting in His promises and trusting in His provision.

Faith-Based Planning

"Now faith is being sure of what we hope for and certain of what we do not see. This is what the ancients were commended for." (Hebrews 11:1-2)

Unlike fear-based planning that results in paralysis, or fact-based planning that results in blindness, faith-based planning results in commendation! Faith is what God commended the ancients for, and faith is what God commends us for.

But it's not easy, is it? Fear can overcome us and facts can overwhelm us, and when either happens, faith takes a backseat. As you read through *Faith-Based*, you'll encounter a variety of processes and tools to help ensure that your plans are rooted in faith, rather than fear or fact.

COUNT THE COST; COUNT THE LOSS

A word of caution as you plan: Count the cost! Don't overlook that when we step out in faith, there is always sacrifice, and we are wise to count the cost before we step too far (Luke 14:28).

Conversely, we must also count the loss as we plan. By that I mean that we need to consider the consequences of knowing what we ought to do, but failing to do it, or even plan for it (Ephesians 5:15-16). Just as there is a cost when taking a step for God, so too is there loss - in the form of lost opportunity - when we fail to step out in faith. This ought to garner our attention, especially in light of James 4:17: "If anyone, then, knows the good they ought to do and doesn't do it, it is sin for them."

ROLES AND RESPONSIBILITIES

As you prepare to plan, it is important to clearly delineate roles and responsibilities. A basic summary is provided below, and serves as a healthy guideline. [4]

> *Jesus Christ*: Head of the Church; calls us to mission; inspires our vision.
> *Elders and Deacons:* Govern the mission.
> *Pastor(s):* Lead the mission; inspire, train, and teach.
> *Staff:* Manage the ministry; equip the congregation.
> *Congregation:* Ministers; carry out the mission.

Jesus is our Head, and all we do and say must point back to who Christ is, and what He has done (and is doing). Jesus gives us a common mission and inspires a unique vision.

The role of elders and deacons is critical! Pastors come and go, but elders and deacons tend to stay much longer. They provide continuity while working to ensure that the mission remains priority one at all times, and during all seasons.

Pastors lead the mission and raise up leaders who will partner in leading as well. The staff manages the ministry and equips the congregation to carry out ministry. Each congregant is to be a minister, called by God to carry out the mission God has placed on His people, and His church.

PLANNING CYCLE AND ALIGNMENT MODEL

Strategic planning in the church is a delicate undertaking! If you establish a viable planning process and simply repeat it year over year, your planning will quickly become stale, predictable, and uninspiring, with little or no room to think creatively and be led by the Holy Spirit. On the other hand, if you introduce a new planning process every year, your planning will lack continuity and cohesion, and will instead bring about chaos and uncertainty.

Both of these approaches are flawed, but there is a third approach that takes the best of both: Begin by establishing a *basic framework* that lends itself to a viable, repeatable planning process, and then be intentional to allow ample room for creativity, and for seeking and following the leading of the Holy Spirit. It's simple but highly effective.

The planning cycle and alignment model stem from many years of working to create a church planning process that is effective and repeatable, yet allows plenty of space for creativity and discerning the leading of the Holy Spirit.

Planning Cycle

The planning cycle is built around the six sections of *Faith-Based*, and while aggressive, has proven to be feasible with a focused effort and strong leadership commitment. The diagram that follows assumes that a church has already established its mission, vision, and values. If that is not the case, take as much time as you need to define these core elements prior to annual planning.

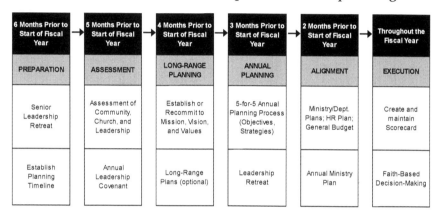

6 Months Prior to Start of Fiscal Year	5 Months Prior to Start of Fiscal Year	4 Months Prior to Start of Fiscal Year	3 Months Prior to Start of Fiscal Year	2 Months Prior to Start of Fiscal Year	Throughout the Fiscal Year
PREPARATION	ASSESSMENT	LONG-RANGE PLANNING	ANNUAL PLANNING	ALIGNMENT	EXECUTION
Senior Leadership Retreat	Assessment of Community, Church, and Leadership	Establish or Recommit to Mission, Vision, and Values	5-for-5 Annual Planning Process (Objectives, Strategies)	Ministry/Dept. Plans; HR Plan; General Budget	Create and maintain Scorecard
Establish Planning Timeline	Annual Leadership Covenant	Long-Range Plans (optional)	Leadership Retreat	Annual Ministry Plan	Faith-Based Decision-Making

I recommend that during the *Preparation* phase, senior leaders (pastors and a few other key leaders) spend a day together to pray and invite the Holy Spirit to lead them individually, and as a church, as they enter into a season of planning. A senior leadership retreat is ideal for recommitting to the mission given *by* Christ, pledging unity with one another *in* Christ, and agreeing to seek the leading of the Holy Spirit for *the cause* of Christ. A senior leadership retreat is also ideal for establishing an overall project plan, with key milestones, roles and responsibilities, meeting dates, etc.

Alignment Model

While there is flexibility in defining a planning framework, we must always start with the Great Commission and Great Commandment. All that we do must flow from, and point back to, Jesus' commission and command for us.

God's Great Commission and Great Commandment

All of our plans must align with and support the Great Commission and Commandment.

↓ ↑

Mission

The mission answers the question of why we exist. It equates to God's call – God's purpose – for the church, and comes directly from the Great Commission given us by Christ. Leadership must revisit and recast the mission often to ensure ongoing focus and attainment.

↓ ↑

Vision

The vision answers the question of what God is leading us to be in the future to fulfill the mission, and when we project (or at least hope) the vision will come to fruition. Vision is often more directional than specific, but at all times is a sort of picture of how we sense God leading and calling us going forward. Leadership must not only cast the vision, but live in accordance with the vision.

↓ ↑

Values

Our values answer the question of what we will endeavor to safeguard in and through all circumstances and at all times. In essence, our values are what define us; what make us who we are. Values should be over-arching rather than tactical or situational. Values should be revisited annually to either reaffirm or adjust.

↓ ↑

Long-Range Plans (LRPs)

LRPs serve as a bridge between the vision, which is typically 5-7 years from coming to fruition, and objectives, which are established annually. LRPs require at least 2 years, and as many as 5 years, to complete. Establishing LRPs is optional during the planning cycle, but if LRPs exist, they should be revisited and reassessed annually.

↓ ↑

Objectives

Annual objectives answer the question of what God is leading us to do in the coming year to be faithful to the mission, step toward the vision, and uphold our values. Objectives are established annually, communicated regularly and creatively to the congregation, and should be at least somewhat measurable. Objectives must clearly align with mission, vision, and values.

↓ ↑

Strategies

Strategies answer the question of what we will do in the coming year to achieve the objectives. Typically, strategies are set annually in conjunction with establishing objectives. Strategies can be altered, stopped, or added throughout the year as the Holy Spirit leads and guides.

↓ ↑

Ministry/Department Plans

Ministry/Department Plans are the individual plans from

each ministry and department. These plans are typically set by staff and answer the question of how our ministries and departments, in the coming year, will help fulfill the mission, step toward the vision, and support the objectives and strategies.

↓ ↑

Human Resources (HR) Plan

The HR Plan delineates people, positions, and responsibilities. The HR Plan should represent what we believe to be optimal stewardship of the staff (and possibly key volunteers) that God has brought to us. Most often, the HR Plan entails minor adjustments to position and/or job scope, but at times more significant changes are necessary.

↓ ↑

Budget

The budget must align with and support all that we do. The budget must be developed with ample prayer and steadfast commitment to good stewardship. The budget, as with all of our plans, must be faith-based and held loosely.

QUESTIONS FOR DISCUSSION & REFLECTION

* How do you typically plan? How does your church typically plan?

* What holds you back from planning?

* Why is our gravitational pull toward fear-based and/or fact-based planning?

- How might we increasingly gravitate toward a faith-based planning approach?

- Ask your leadership team for their assessment relative to which planning approach your church has used in the past. Is there any correlation between your approach to planning and the extent of God's blessing and provision upon the church? (Caution: Be very, very careful here! God provides all that we need according to His good will and purpose, not according to what we think we need. Don't make this a transaction! All we bring to the table is faith, and God alone brings the increase. This question is intended simply to uncover any patterns where the blessing and provision of God may be more prevalent in certain seasons than others).

2

TRUE NORTH

Any planning we do in the church is an exercise in futility if we don't begin by reaffirming and embracing the supremacy of Christ, and the centrality of the Gospel. For believers, and for churches, this must be our "true north," the singular point we journey toward.

But what is true in our lives is also true when it comes to how we plan, and how we execute our plans – namely, that we are prone to wander ... *a lot*. Sometimes we veer far off course, but most often our wandering is subtle, by degrees. We're still traveling north – our ministries are functional, our programs robust, most of our congregants seem content, even growing – but we're not traveling *true* north.

Because whereas true north is focused on the supremacy and Gospel of Jesus Christ above all else, in our flesh we are prone to shift our focus off of Christ and on to other things during both times of crisis and times of prosperity. In both cases, we easily lose our sense of who God is and who we are as His people, and begin to function on our own strength. That's why it's so important for all Christians, but especially for church pastors and leaders, to regularly reaffirm the supremacy of Christ and the centrality of the Gospel, and to filter our plans and decisions accordingly.

THE SUPREMACY OF CHRIST

"The Son is the image of the invisible God, the firstborn over all creation. For in him all things were created: things in heaven and on earth, visible and invisible, whether thrones or powers or rulers or authorities; all things have been created through him and for him. He is before all things, and in him all things hold together. And he is the head of the body, the church; he is the beginning and the firstborn from among the dead, so that in everything he might have the supremacy. For God was pleased to have all his fullness dwell in him, and through him to reconcile to himself all things, whether things on earth or things in heaven, by making peace through his blood, shed on the cross." (Colossians 1:15-20)

To affirm the supremacy of Christ is to affirm that Jesus Christ is God. Jesus has dominion over all, and is above all. Jesus alone can forgive sin and reconcile people back to God. [5]

THE CENTRALITY OF THE GOSPEL

The Gospel must be central to all that we do, say, and think. The truth of the Gospel – God's unfathomable love (John 3:16, Romans 5:8), our inherent sin (Romans 3:23, 5:12), salvation by and through Jesus Christ (Romans 6:23, John 1:12) – is the Good News that we are called to live out and carry to the very ends of the earth.

Straightforward? Yes! But easy to stand firm in? Not so much.

The truth is that standing firm – and I mean really standing firm, as in being squared, centered, immovable in the Gospel - doesn't come easy, nor does it come naturally. And the real kicker is this: The biggest problem we have when it comes to standing firm in the Gospel is ourselves.

Here's how author Michael Horton describes the problem:

> "In such a therapeutic, pragmatic, pull yourself up by your bootstraps society as ours, the message of God having to do all the work in saving us comes as an offensive shot at our egos. In this culture, religion is all about being good, about the horizontal, about loving God and neighbor. But all of that is the fruit of the gospel. The gospel has nothing to do with what I do. The gospel is entirely a message about what someone else has done not only for me but also for the renewal of the whole creation." [6]

Horton's words are direct and to the point, but if you're a visual person, here are two illustrations that reinforce the truth of the Gospel:

In the Gospel diagram at left, God allowed His only Son, Jesus Christ, to descend to us. Jesus lived a perfect life, suffered, died and was buried, and three days later rose from the grave and now sits at the right hand of God the Father. Jesus alone can break the power of sin and death that separates us from God. This is the Gospel, and it's *all* about God's descension to us.

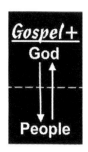

But the slippery slope that Horton is referring to is what he terms "Gospel Plus." Here, there's an understanding that God did in fact descend in Christ to save us, but added to that is a belief that to be truly reconciled to God we must also somehow, someway "ascend" to God. In the early church, the tendency was to add in Old Testament Law, which of course diluted the true Gospel. And while today we don't mix Law with the Gospel, we do tend to add in things like good deeds, religiosity, and self-actualization.

But *anything* we add to the Gospel of Jesus Christ results in a hybrid, diluted Gospel – Gospel Plus. So why do we tend to veer in this direction so easily? Mostly because it's just plain less offensive to us. That's why we're drawn to alternative forms of the Gospel, and why it's so important to reaffirm on a regular basis the centrality of the true Gospel of Jesus Christ.

Here's another reason we must stay rooted in the Gospel ...

"A little yeast works through the whole batch of dough." (Galatians 5:9)

What Paul is doing here is simply echoing Jesus' words of warning from Matthew 16:6, when Jesus told His disciples to, "Be on your guard against the yeast of the Pharisees and Sadducees." The thing about yeast is that it's an actual living organism. If you add a touch of yeast to a batch of dough, it changes the dough's shape and flavor – for better or worse. In Galatia, Paul knew that some bad yeast had begun to quickly and actively permeate and spoil four churches that until that point had been rooted in the perfect yeast of the Gospel.

Can this happen today? Does this happen today? It can, and it does. And it can be argued that "bad yeast" is the single biggest reason for the ongoing struggle of the American church. Because it doesn't take much more than a pinch of legalism, or a pinch of pluralism, or a pinch of rules and customs mandated by people rather than scripture, or a pinch of compromise on essential biblical doctrine, or a pinch of being program-driven rather than Gospel-driven, or a pinch of this or that or the other thing, before the "dough" of a church becomes altered and bland. And it's bad enough when bad yeast permeates the dough of a single church, but when bunches of churches, or even entire denominations, are permeated by bad yeast, well, Houston, we've got a problem.

As God's people, and as the Church of Jesus Christ, we have a responsibility to stand firm when it comes to not allowing bad yeast to enter into our churches. Keeping the Gospel – the true, unfiltered, undiluted Gospel of Jesus Christ – central to all that we do, say, and think, is of the utmost importance.

QUESTIONS FOR DISCUSSION & REFLECTION

- What is it that prompts you to shift your focus off of Christ and on to something (or someone) else? Do you sense any patterns?

- If your congregants were surveyed, what might they say is the single most important aspect of the church?

- Spend some time wrestling with the questions above. Be honest about where you are at personally, and where your church is at as a whole. Pray for clarity and conviction on this topic as you prepare to enter into a planning season.

3

PLANNING LANDMINES

As with any process, there are many landmines to be aware of, and to avoid, when planning. The list below comes from experience. I have personally encountered, and at times struggled with, each of these landmines. And while experience is a good teacher, so too is avoidance! Learn from my mistakes, and do all you can to avoid stepping on these planning landmines.

Lack of Prayer

I realize that this landmine is rather obvious, but because prayer is so important – essential, actually – it belongs on top of the list. Typically, a lack of prayer isn't an issue at the beginning of a planning process, but when things start to come together and plans are solidified – when we start to feel pretty good about what we think *we've* done – prayer can easily wane. Prayer also tends to get pushed to the backburner when we are overwhelmed with the tyranny of the urgent; when everything feels like a crisis. Stephen Covey makes the point that the reason most people run out of gas while driving is that they feel they're too busy to stop for gas! [7] Prayer is fuel – we need it to be fully alive, fully engaged, and fully surrendered.

Lack of Faith

Even when our plans have been bathed in prayer and well discerned, they can at times seem too distant, too big, and just plain too much. Starting in faith is important, but remaining in faith is even more so.

Holding our plans loosely is important (which is why "inflexibility" is listed as a planning landmine), but so too is trusting God to overcome whatever obstacles may come our way. Indeed, if our plans have been established through seeking and being obedient to the leading of the Holy Spirit, then we must trust God to do what only He can.

For a vivid reminder of God's sovereignty, read God's speech to Job in Job 38-41, which begins with, "Who is this that obscures my plans with words without knowledge?"[8] And for a vivid reminder of how we ought to respond to God's sovereignty, read Job's reply to God in Job 42, which begins with, "I know that you can do all things; no purpose of yours can be thwarted."[9]

Failure to add Wisdom to Faith

Just as a lack of faith is a landmine, so too is a failure to add wisdom to faith. God has given you a unique mix of gifts, skills, and experiences. And God has given you *His* wisdom, expressed in the Scriptures. And if all of that isn't enough, God has even given you Himself through the gift of the Holy Spirit. Active prayer and steadfast faith are essential, but don't overlook the importance of wisdom as well.

Overlooking the Reality of Spiritual Warfare

If you and other leaders at your church earnestly seek to be led by the Holy Spirit, and are willing to follow the Sprit's leading at all costs, you will experience spiritual warfare, demonic attack. The bible makes this clear, and experience makes it tangible. And make no mistake, you have a choice in this. You can go through the motions, content to be "good enough," which pretty much guarantees that you won't need to deal with spiritual warfare.

Or, you can seek and follow God's leading for whatever might come, understanding that in doing so you will experience spiritual warfare. If its comfort you're after, take the first option; but if your desire is to be part of advancing the Kingdom of God on earth, then enter in with gusto, and be sure to wear the full armor of God (Ephesians 6:13-18) at all times.

Failure to Celebrate

Is this really a landmine? Yes! Celebrating the movement of God - in people, churches, and communities - blesses God while orienting us toward God. We need to be intentional to notice ways God is at work, and even more intentional about giving God all the glory. Celebrations have a way of reminding us that it's not about what we do, but what God is doing in us, through us, and at times in spite of us.

Planning Fatigue

Planning requires a significant investment in prayer, focus, time, and resources. The operative word here is *investment*, because if we fully commit to a biblical planning process, and if we see it through, the benefits will far outweigh the sacrifices. But without question, planning is fatiguing, and the temptation to check out is strong. Allow yourself to take a break from time to time, but be careful to do so without compromising the overall planning process. A rhythm of steady advancement followed by temporary pause and celebration is ideal.

Inflexibility

When it comes to planning, one of the most significant inducers of stress comes when we hold our plans (or even our approach to planning) so tight that we refuse to let go. No one sets out to make an idol out of a plan, but it happens all too frequently. Usually, it's as simple as a person latching on to what seems to be the right way – the *only* way – to do something, and closing himself off to other thoughts or ideas. The counter to this is to hold our plans loose, inviting the Holy Spirit to redirect our plans according to His leading.

Procrastination

You've heard the saying, "I have met the enemy, and the enemy is me!" If you are prone to procrastination – and you know who you are – than you must establish a timeline and be accountable for meeting it. Procrastination stalls momentum, and ultimately kills a planning process. Be aware of, and be honest about, your own tendencies, and ask others to hold you accountable to a timeline.

People Pleasing

For many leaders, this represents the most threatening landmine of all. We know that we are to work for God rather than people

(Col. 3:23), and that capitulation to the demands of people is a dangerous trap (Proverbs 29:25), yet most of us struggle in this area. I recommend that you make an honest commitment before God, and before other leaders, to avoid this landmine at all costs – with God's help, and with the help and support of the leaders God has surrounded you with. Without question, if you prayerfully, faithfully, and earnestly enter into a planning season, you will emerge with God-sized plans that will threaten the status quo.

As a leader, you will reach a point (actually several points) when you will need to choose between pleasing God, and pleasing people. Be sure to surround yourself with people who will support you by their words, actions, and prayers. Just as Moses needed Aaron and Hur to hold his arms up to defeat the Amalekite army, so too will you need people to hold your arms up to defeat the temptation to please people, rather than God.

QUESTIONS FOR DISCUSSION & REFLECTION

- Which of the planning landmines are you most susceptible to? What can you do now to help ensure that you don't fall victim to planning landmines later?

- Which landmines have you struggled with in the past?

- Are there landmines that you are prone to struggle with that aren't listed here?

PART TWO

ASSESSMENT

Assessment is the equivalent of holding up a mirror and taking a long, hard look at who we *really* are, and how we *really* function. It's not easy, and trying to stay objective is an ongoing challenge, especially when everything feels personal.

My hope and prayer is that the thoughts and ideas presented in this section, along with the "key tools" provided later, will both spur and enable you to successfully work through a season of assessment.

A simple internal assessment using the *Spiritual Farming Template* and/or *Deep and Wide Exercise* can be a gateway to a rich, soul searching journey of discovery. However, a comprehensive external assessment can bring objectivity and clarity in ways that an internal assessment cannot.

A good rule of thumb is to work through one or both of the *Faith-Based* assessment tools annually, and to undergo a more comprehensive external assessment every three to five years.

4

GOSPEL AND CULTURE

"How, then, can they call on the one they have not believed in? And how can they believe in the one whom they have not heard? And how can they hear without someone preaching to them?"
Romans 10:14

The Gospel brings meaning to life, and light to darkness. The Gospel is powerful, encompassing, unifying, and life changing. And as pastors and leaders in Christ's church, the Gospel must always be at the very center of all that we do, say, and think.

We know this to be true, yet we also know that what we do with the Gospel – *how* we bring the Gospel to people – can be, at times, confounding. Because while the Gospel is unchanging, the people we are called to bring the Gospel to are anything but. Nations differ, regions differ, neighborhoods differ, families differ, people differ! What resonates in one culture is offensive in another; what sparks passion in one person spurs anger in another person.

I recall a Human Genome lecture I attended several years ago where the speaker said that because no two people are alike, each person is in essence a unique culture unto him or herself. So, how exactly do we go about trying to reach over seven billion people, all of whom are unique in countless ways, with the singular, all-encompassing Gospel of Jesus Christ?

Thankfully, no single person or church bears the burden of reaching seven billion people, but we are called to reach people we are in proximity to, and to actively support global missions. And beyond reaching people for Christ, we are to help people become more like Christ. Our call is to venture both wide *("Go ...")* and deep *("... and make Disciples")* – in combination.

Easy enough, right? Umm, not so much! But we do it because we want people to have the same assurance we have, and to experience the same journey we are on - a slow, steady, and at times sideways march toward becoming who God created us to be. We do it because we know that only Christ can set a person free from the stronghold of sin, and the permanence of death. We do it because we want what is ultimately best for people, and we get frustrated when they don't see what we see, and don't grasp what we grasp.

But I wonder if we're working out of the wrong paradigm. I wonder what would happen if instead of trying to figure out why people don't see what we see, we took the time to try to figure out what they see – their interests, their fears, their beliefs, their doubts, their values, their circumstances ... their *culture*. Because if it's true that the Gospel is for all people, then it's equally true that any success we have in advancing the Gospel message is very much tied to our understanding of, and willingness to engage, people in their own unique setting – in their own unique culture.

My belief is that a primary reason for churches (and pastors and leaders) not being more effective in both outreach and discipleship is a common propensity to discount the significance of culture. Yes, the Gospel is unchanging, but culture is *constantly* changing.

This brings us to the crux of the problem, namely that most of us aren't adequately tuned in to the culture around us. Is this important? Vitally so. And it's biblical too – Paul carried the same Gospel wherever he went, but how he presented it varied according to the culture he was seeking to reach. But what about us? The truth is that most of us aren't sure how to engage the culture, or even whether it's appropriate to engage the culture. And certainly, assimilation for the sake of assimilation isn't the answer, but ignoring the culture altogether isn't either. Can we find a middle ground, one where the Gospel is proclaimed and advanced in ways that meet people where they're at, instead of where we think they ought to be?

Tim Keller addresses this question (and many others) in his brilliant book, *Center Church: Doing Balanced, Gospel-Centered Ministry in Your City*.[10] Keller affirms the centrality of the Gospel, but makes the point that Gospel movement is contingent on appropriate engagement with the culture. Keller points out that if we overadapt to a culture, we won't change people because we won't call them to change, and that if we underadapt to a culture, no one will be changed because no one will listen to us.

Finding the right balance, the right middle ground, between overadapting and underadapting to a culture is worth striving for, and worth revisiting at least annually as part of a planning process. It's worth striving for because when the power – the movement – of the Gospel sweeps through people and churches, the surrounding culture can't help but be swept up as well. And as Christians, we have it in us to spur this kind of *movement*, not on our own, but as called and equipped ambassadors for Christ.

How do you change a culture? You look to Jesus …

CULTURE SHIFT

Recalling the earlier point that in essence every person is a culture unto him or herself, let us consider the "culture" of Christ ...

> "The Word became flesh and made his dwelling among us." (John 1:14a)

Jesus was *fully present*.

> "We have seen his glory, the glory of the one and only Son, who came from the Father, full of grace and truth."
> (John 1:14b)

Jesus was a *giver of grace* and a *teller of truth* – grace and truth were as two sides of the same coin for Christ, with no incompatibility whatsoever.

> "The Son of Man did not come to be served, but to serve..."
> (Matthew 20:28)

Jesus always put others ahead of Himself; Jesus came to *serve*.

> "For I have come down from heaven not to do my will but to do the will of him who sent me." (John 6:38)

Jesus was *willingly obedient* to the Father.

We can find many other verses in Scripture that speak to the "culture" of Jesus, but these verses are sufficient to demonstrate how Jesus can shift a culture simply by being who He is, and meeting people where they are at.

Surely you are familiar with the story of Jesus' encounter with a Samaritan woman at Jacob's well. But have you studied the story through the eyes of culture – the culture of Christ, the culture of Samaria, and the culture of the woman herself?

We know about Jesus' culture – that Jesus was fully present, filled with both grace and truth, a servant, willingly obedient - but what about the culture of Samaria? Samaritans were a mixed race who were hated and considered impure by the Jews, so much so that they would do all they could to avoid having to travel through Samaria. And practically speaking, getting water from a well was hard work! The wells were normally located outside the city along the main road, and women would typically go for water twice each day, morning and evening.

But let's not stop there; let's also consider the "culture" of the woman herself. Because if getting water wasn't hard enough, for her it must have been brutal. Indeed, based on her reputation, she came to the well at noon to avoid people who might know her. She was ostracized – a person despised by people who were themselves despised.

I'd like you to pause for a few minutes to read John 4:4-42. But read it through the eyes of culture. Imagine what the woman must have experienced when Jesus addresses her; imagine the townspeople as the woman shares her story. And mostly, take note of how the culture of Christ intersects with both the culture of the woman and the town in Samaria.

∞∞

You can't miss it, can you? Jesus changed a life by simply being who He is, and being willing to engage a person right where she was at, in all of her messiness and dysfunction. If the story ended there it would be worth sharing, but it gets better still as this courageous woman leaves her water jar behind and tells the people, "Come, see a man who told me everything I ever did. Could this be the Messiah?"[11] And so they came, and many believed, and to this day we stand amazed at what took place at a lonely well in Samaria in the middle of a hot, dry day.

What does the story mean for us? It means that authentic, lasting culture change, the kind that won't spoil or perish or fade, begins with Christ. He is the One who ultimately brings about transformation, simply by being who He is, and doing what He does. Jesus is sufficient.

It means that because of what Christ has done for us and the gift of the Holy Spirit in us, we have it in us to become increasingly more like Christ, and to reflect the "culture" of Christ in all places, at all times.

It means that, like the Samaritan woman, we are ambassadors for Christ, and must be courageous to value the Gospel over tradition.

It means that while plans are good, anything we do is incomplete in the absence of Christ ... because authentic, sustainable culture change not only starts with Christ, it remains rooted and centered in Christ.

Finally, it means that if we are willing to understand and appropriately engage the surrounding culture, we will share in the joy of seeing more and more people come to Christ, and grow to be more like Christ.

QUESTIONS FOR DISCUSSION & REFLECTION

- How would you describe the culture of your congregation? Your community?

- How are you doing at bringing the Gospel message to people in both your church and community in ways that meet them where they are at?

- What is your tendency – to overadapt to culture, or to underadapt to culture? (Explain)

- What adjustments might you need to make in how you bring the unchanging Gospel to an ever-changing culture?

5

SPIRITUAL FARMING, PART ONE

Let me begin with a confession: Not only am I not a farmer, I'm not even a gardener! In fact, at this very moment, I am examining my fingernails, and cannot find even one speck of dirt underneath. Not only that, but I can't seem to find even a hint of green on my thumb! Now don't get me wrong – I *appreciate* both a good farm and a good garden, and I'm grateful that my wife actually does have a green thumb - but working the land is just not my thing. So there's my confession, which adds nothing, but feels oddly therapeutic to me.

Conventional farming holds no appeal whatsoever for me, but *spiritual farming* has the opposite effect. What do I mean by "spiritual farming?" Simply that just as producing an abundant harvest is the goal of conventional farming, so too is it the goal of spiritual farming. Not a harvest of fruit or vegetables, but of fully devoted followers - disciples - of Jesus Christ.

References to both conventional and spiritual farming appear in various places throughout scripture, perhaps most notably in the Parable of the Sower (Mark 4:1-20, Matthew 13:1-23, Luke 8:1-15). After Jesus gave the parable to a large crowd, He later gave a brief explanation of the parable to His disciples, giving them just enough to enable them to explore its deeper meaning and application.

Now, I have no idea if Jesus' disciples actually went on to explore the parable's deeper meaning and application, but I am reasonably certain that most Christians fail to take that extra step. And this is unfortunate, because we have it in us to go deeper with the parables (and, for that matter, with the whole of scripture).

David Guzik explains that, "Parables, in their spiritual function, are more like riddles or puzzles than easy illustrations. They can be understood by those who have right 'key.'"

In the Parable of the Sower, the key Guzik speaks of is the "secret" Jesus refers to in Mark 4:11, when he told the Disciples that, "The secret of the kingdom of God has been given to you. But to those on the outside everything is said in parables ..."

In other words, all who are followers of Jesus Christ already have the key – the secret of the Kingdom of God – because the key is Christ Himself, the Word of God incarnate. The key opens the door to ... well, to everything. But we decide whether or not to enter in.

Guzik offers these additional words of wisdom: "When Jesus used parables, He didn't start by stating a truth. Instead, the parable was like a doorway. Jesus' listeners stood at the doorway and heard Him. If they were not interested, they stayed on the outside. But if they were interested, they could walk through the doorway, and think more about the truth behind the parable and what it meant to their life." [12]

So how about it? Will you join me in walking through the doorway that takes us deeper into thinking about how the Parable of the Sower, and farming in general, can enhance our understanding of and success in strategic planning?

It seems to me that the best way to get started is to create a sort of tapestry between what we can glean from the Parable of the Sower, and from a conventional farming process, and how both inform and bring enlightenment to "spiritual farming." The approach here might seem odd, but I hope you stay with me because there are some amazing lessons to be gleaned.

We could choose just about any kind of fruit or vegetable (sorry, no livestock today), but seeing as though just yesterday I received a surprise gift from a co-worker of a trio of plump, juicy, exceedingly delicious oranges, I am inclined to go the way of the orange.

GROWING ORANGES; GROWING DISCIPLES

Climate; Roots

The first thing to know about growing oranges is that orange trees will only grow in warm areas, which in the United States means the south (so *that's* why I've never seen an orange tree in Michigan). And it probably goes without saying that oranges like sun, and lots of it.

Just as climate is a major factor for growing oranges, so too is climate a major factor when growing disciples. In the Parable of the Sower, after Jesus begins with a farmer sowing seed along a path and on rocky places, He makes this statement:

> "But when the sun came up, the plants were scorched, and they withered because they had no root" (Mark 4:6).

47

When the climate became hot, when the sun beat down with its full intensity, the roots of the plants – *the roots of the people* – weren't deep enough to avoid getting scorched, withered.

Jesus is describing a universal challenge, one that all Christians have experienced and can relate to. Each of us have gone through times, even prolonged seasons, of pronounced strife and challenge ... times when we feel as if we are trapped under the sun on a hot afternoon in the middle of July, with no shade in sight; times when the roots - the depth – of our faith makes all the difference in determining whether the heat causes us to wither, or spurs us to grow.

The climate we are exposed to has a significant impact on our lives, but more than that, it has a significant impact on whole churches. In fact, whether you realize it or not, your church has a climate, and it's a climate unlike any other church in the world. And your climate is not only unique to your church, it's unique to this exact point in time. The climate of your church can and will change, sometimes slow and subtly, sometimes quickly and dramatically, and more often than not, unexpectedly.

To illustrate the point, imagine that you begin a new call to pastor a church. You come in loaded with energy, ideas and sermons, and people are excited. In fact, they keep telling you that you're exactly what the church has needed, and that finally – *finally* – things are turning around for the better. The climate of the church has moved from partly cloudy to mostly sunny, and by golly, pretty soon it'll be seventy-five and sunny every day! But slowly ... slowly ... the climate changes. The energy on Sunday mornings seems somehow less; those ideas you came in with seemed great, at least until people started to figure out that doing something new meant stopping something comfortable; and now you're hearing rumblings that some members would prefer that you spend less time challenging people to change, and more time telling them that Jesus loves them just as they are. The climate has changed; the heat is rising. Are your roots deep enough to withstand intense, even scorching heat? You're about to find out.

If that scenario doesn't resonate with you, try this one: You attend a conference, one so powerful, so provocative, that you come back fired up and ready to lead your congregation into a new season, a season you just know will bring many people to Christ, and grow many people to become more like Christ. Your enthusiasm is contagious, so much so that in short order the staff and consistory of the church are nodding their heads in agreement and ready to join you in this super amazing, ultra-mega life changing initiative. And so it starts ... and stalls. To your dismay, the congregation doesn't seem nearly as enthusiastic about this initiative as you are, or for that matter as your staff and leaders are. Soon you begin to feel like Moses, hoping against hope that the church will finally "get it" at some point, yet resigned that the next big thing is going to end up being just another failed attempt to breathe new life into dry bones. And so you have a decision to make: Do you stay with the initiative and try to make it work, knowing that the climate of the church is about to get very, very hot? Or do you turn down the heat by pulling away from the initiative?

Hopefully these examples are helpful in showing how much climate effects people, pastors, and churches. There are, of course, numerous other examples that make the point, none more so than the real life experiences you have faced (or are facing) while in ministry.

But let's bear in mind that while climate is critically important, it's only one of many variables in a farming process. In fact, in the Parable of the Sower, don't lose sight of the fact that it wasn't the climate – the heat - that caused the plants to wither, it was that the plants had insufficient roots. In our lives, and in our churches, we *will* have trouble – Jesus said so, we know so – which means that the real question is not whether we will face intense heat (we will), but whether we're sufficiently rooted to withstand the heat.

As climate relates to spiritual farming, what I most want you to take away is this: Before you go too far in planning, take time to understand the climate of your church and to objectively assess the depth of your roots, as well as those of your leaders and congregation. Think about how much change the church can realistically absorb at one time; think about what the right pace of change might be for the church; think about what an ideal climate might be at your church to produce growth, not in one fell swoop but growth that is slow, steady, and sustainable.

If your roots, or the roots of your leaders, or the roots of the congregation, aren't deep enough to withstand long periods of high heat, then do the wise thing - plan in such a way that you adjust the climate *gradually*, by degrees, rather than all at once. Let your roots grow and expand, making gradual climate adjustments along the way. Just as there are many kinds of oranges, each with their own unique flavor, so too are there many kinds of disciples, and many kinds of churches, each with their own unique flavor. Do what works for your church. And remember, slow growth beats scorched and withered every time.

Soil

Having the right soil is crucial for growing a healthy, fruitful orange tree. The soil should ideally be neutral to slightly acidic, and well drained. High clay content is better than sandy soil, which requires much more frequent watering and fertilizing. And adding organic content such as compost is helpful for enhancing water and nutrient holding ability in all soil.

In the Parable of the Sower, the farmer sows seed on four different types of soil, with varying results. He begins by scattering seed along a path – hard, trodden soil where nothing can grow – and the seed is quickly devoured by birds. Jesus later explains that this represents people who hear the word but don't understand it, and lose what little understanding they have. This, not coincidentally, is one of Satan's goals (2 Corinthians 4:3-4).

Do you recognize this kind of soil in your church? Soil that has been trampled over so many times, soil that is so barren and hard, that nothing can possibly grow there?

Just as recognizing the climate of your church is important, so too is recognizing the soil of your church. If the church cares more about traditions, customs, history, and protocol than making disciples, then the soil of the church is hard and trampled, not conducive to growth.

The good news is that if you do have hard, trampled soil, you can take steps to alter it. I'll have more to say about that shortly, but for now let's continue to think about the soil we find in the Parable of the Sower, and what it holds for us today.

After the farmer scatters seed on the path, he scatters seed on "rocky places," where the soil is shallow. This produces rapid initial growth, but because the soil is shallow, so too are the roots, causing the plant to whither and fall away. Here Jesus is referring to those who, "hear the word and at once receive it with joy. But since they have no root, they last only a short time. When trouble or persecution comes because of the word, they quickly fall away." (Mark 4:16-17).

Where does the problem lie - with the plants that lacked the roots to withstand difficult conditions, or with the soil overrun by rocks?

Remember, we've already established that while we have some control on managing the climate, invariably there will times when it gets scorching hot, and when that happens our ability to avoid withering is dependent on the depth of our roots. But if the soil is shallow – if it's covered by rocks – then the roots *can't* grow deep.

Do you have this kind of soil in your church? Do you have the kind of soil that allows for quick growth, but not ample rooting? Does your church place such a high value on bringing people *to* Christ that it has little or no capacity to help people grow to be more *like* Christ? As a pastor, as a leader, are you passionate about bringing people to faith in Christ, but dispassionate when it comes to the hard work of making disciples?

Many pastors and leaders have unintentionally shrank the Great Commission to a single dimension, one that values conversion over discipleship. This is short-sighted, and needs to be corrected. The Great Commission is meant to be multi-dimensional and all-encompassing, not one-dimensional and limited. But to reclaim the Great Commission in all of its beauty, in all of its fullness, we need to clear away the rocks that are covering the soil of our churches. We'll touch on how to do that in a bit, but let's first continue to think about other types of soil.

The third soil Jesus mentions was chock full of thorns, which grew up and choked the plants. Jesus explains that this represents those who hear the word but allow the worries of this life, the deceitfulness of wealth, and the desire for other things to come in and choke the word, making it unfruitful.

This type of soil is *very* common in churches. The soil starts well, but the small thorns mixed into the soil are allowed to grow, and in due time the thorns overwhelm the soil and eventually choke the life out of the plants - out of the people. The problem is not that the thorns were there to begin with, but that they were never removed, and instead were allowed to grow.

Is the soil of your church overrun with thorns of worry, or disproportionate financial focus, or preoccupation with non-essential things? Are *you* overrun with thorns of worry, or disproportionate financial focus, or preoccupation with non-essential things?

Pay careful attention to what gets discussed at your leadership meetings. If you focus more on solving issues, or controlling finances, or thinking about what the church down the road is doing, than on making disciples, you have thorns in your soil.

But the issue isn't so much the thorns in your soil, it's what you do (or don't do) about the thorns in your soil. Ignoring thorns only causes them to grow; removing thorns takes energy, diligence, and perseverance ... but allows the soil to become healthy, able to yield a harvest.

This brings us to the fourth soil mentioned in the parable: "good" soil, soil that allowed the seed to come to fruition and produce an abundant harvest, thirty-fold, sixty-fold, even a hundred-fold.

That's the soil we long for, isn't it? Soil so good, so ideal for growth that the crop it produces is *astonishingly* abundant! So what makes for "good" soil? Well, we know that *bad* soil is soil that is hard and packed down, or covered by rocks, or overrun with thorns, so it stands to reason that good soil is absent each of these bad elements.

Let's go back to oranges for a moment. We read earlier that while high clay content is better than sandy soil, growth can still occur in sandy soil if the soil is watered and fertilized more frequently. We also read that adding organic content such as compost helps enhance water and nutrient holding ability.

Are you catching a theme here? "Good" soil doesn't happen by accident; it requires someone to work the land - watering, fertilizing, altering and adding to the soil so that it's ideal to produce an abundant harvest.

Let's think about what this means for our churches ...

How do you alter soil that is packed down and hardened, soil that favors tradition, custom, and protocol over making disciples? You work to soften, to loosen the soil, to move it from hard ground to fertile ground. The problem isn't a lack of soil, but that the soil has been packed down for so many years. The soil can be loosened as you prayerfully discern traditions and customs that have run their course and must stop, and others that simply need a fresh focus and renewed commitment to return to their original meaning and significance. The soil is further loosened as you add in fresh, new ideas and approaches for making disciples.

How do you alter soil that is overrun by rocks, soil that is shallow and unable to support progressive, authentic discipleship? You get rid of the rocks! Don't settle for simply moving the rocks; *remove* the rocks. It's hard, painstaking work, but it's necessary to allow for good soil.

I'll pause here to clarify a key point: If your church does well at bringing people to Christ, by all means don't stop what you are doing! But don't simply add a new discipleship process to what you are already doing, because chances are you'll move from hitting the mark in evangelism and missing the mark in discipleship, to missing the mark in *both* evangelism and discipleship. Why? Because adding – layering – dilutes focus, exhausts resources, and depletes finances. Instead, think carefully about the rocks that you need to remove before adding to your soil.

What are these rocks? Well, basically anything and everything that gets in the way of helping people come to Christ, and to grow more like Christ. *All* of your ministries, programs, and events should in some way either help people enter into new life with Christ, or grow as a disciple of Christ. Anything you do that doesn't help accomplish either of these two aims serves only to take you off mission. They're rocks, and they need to be demolished. But be strategic about how to do this - determine rocks that need to be demolished quickly and swiftly, and take a spiritual sledge hammer to them. But also identify rocks that can be removed slowly and more gradually, as with a ball pein hammer. Do your best to balance urgency with patience, so that the climate of your church doesn't get too hot, too soon.

As for dealing with thorns of worry, or disproportionate financial focus, or preoccupation with non-essential things, my advice is simple: be intentional about looking for thorns, and when you find one, deal with it straight away, before it grows any larger.

How do you remove a spiritual thorn? Well, actually *you* don't – you can't – at least not on your own strength. Spiritual thorns embed themselves so deep within people, and within churches, that they can only come out through deeper surrender to God.

If you, your leaders, or your congregation become consumed with worry, or finances, or anything that doesn't help to make disciples, then pause what you are doing immediately and enter into a pronounced season of prayer, refocusing, and recommitment. Think of it as a fast from thorns that choke the life out of people and churches, if allowed to fester. Be sure to fast by not just giving up bad habits, but replacing them with powerful times of prayer, reflection, and group discussion, allowing God to remove the thorns that have hindered growth.

Seeds

There are essentially two seeding approaches that can be taken to grow an orange tree. The first approach is to use a seed taken directly from an orange. If handled properly, the seed will come to germination after a few weeks, followed by around seven years of "juvenility," in which the tree is non-productive. If the tree survives juvenility, it will become mature, yielding a harvest. Interestingly, when planting a single seed, the likelihood of the resulting tree and fruit being identical to the original tree and fruit is quite low.

The second seeding approach is to plant not an orange seed, but rootstock seed, which allows for a process called "grafting." Grafting is the approach that commercial growers take, and with good reason – grafted trees start producing fruit much sooner than seed planted trees, and unlike seed planted trees, are genetically identical to the parent orange tree. Grafting involves fusing the branches of an orange tree with the rootstock of another tree, chosen by growers for attributes such as disease resistance, rapid root growth, and ideal size.

Hold that thought for a bit while we return to the Parable of the Sower. After the crowd had left, Jesus' disciples asked Him to explain the parables He had been teaching earlier in the day. But rather than explain all of the parables, Jesus explains only one: The Parable of the Sower. Jesus begins by saying, "The farmer sows the word" (Mark 4:14), a clear indication that the "seed" in the parable represents the Word of God. Furthermore, given that Jesus is the Word of God (John 1:1), we can say with assurance that the seed represents Christ as well.

This matters greatly because even if the seed we sow is the very Word of God, as expressed in the 66 canonical books that make up the bible, yet fail to connect the Word of God to the Word who became flesh (John 1:14), the seed we sow will be incomplete.

In Matthew 23:3, Jesus instructed His disciples to obey the Pharisees teaching, but not to do what the Pharisees did. Jesus knew that while the Pharisees could recite and teach the Law of Moses, they had no inclination to live accordingly. And Jesus knew that what the Pharisees spoke from their mouths didn't align with the condition of their hearts. This is why Jesus told His disciples to follow their teaching, but not their actions.

Is it possible for us to be like Pharisees, preaching and teaching the Word of God with knowledge and fervor, but failing to connect the words we speak with the Word made flesh? Or ... is it possible for us to preach and teach the Word of God with our minds, but not allow the Word of God to penetrate our hearts?

Yes ... and yes. Because while the Word of God is perfect, we, alas, are not. The good news, however, is that despite our flaws, God's Word does not return empty, but accomplishes God's will and purposes (Isaiah 55:11). Still, that doesn't excuse us from sowing the full, rich seed of the Word of God.

The Word of God is true, absolutely so, but more than that, the Word is living and active, able to change us, conform us, make us more like Christ. To preach and teach from that place – from a mind that has been renewed, a heart that has been changed – is to sow seed that reflects the fullness of God's Word … and of Christ Himself. *That's* the seed we must sow!

Incidentally, lest there be any confusion, let us establish that as a pastor, as a leader, *you* are the farmer, the one who scatters the seed of God's Word. And so the question isn't so much whether you are sowing the seed of God's Word (I assume you are), but whether you are embodying the seed that you are sowing. If Jesus were physically present at your church, would He instruct your congregants to follow your teaching, but not to do what you do? This is a hard question to wrestle with, but I hope you will.

There is a second question that emerges relative to sowing the seed of God's Word, and it relates to the type of *approach* taken at your church.

Think back for a moment to the two seeding approaches that can be taken to grow orange trees. The first approach involved a single seed, which if properly planted and nurtured, could produce a mature, fruitful tree in around seven years, albeit with a low likelihood of matching the original tree. The second approach was to selectively graft the rootstock from one tree onto another tree, allowing for rapid growth and, surprisingly, a tree identical to its parent. So… which seeding approach do you take at your church?

If the seed you sow is strictly a Sunday morning sermon sort of seed, then my advice is to be prepared to wait (and wait and wait and wait) before juvenility gives way to maturity. Because while the seed you sow on Sunday may bear fruit, the process will be like growing an orange tree with a single seed – slow, strenuous, and unpredictable.

On the other hand, if the seeding approach you take at your church is to utilize grafting wherever and whenever possible, then you already know the joy of seeing rapid growth that consistently produces fully devoted followers of Jesus Christ.

Here are some questions to help you distinguish which seeding approach – single seed or grafting – your church employs at the present time. If your answer to the majority of the questions below is "no," then your seeding approach is primarily "single seed"; if the answer is "yes," then your seeding approach is primarily one of grafting:

1. Is there a built-in expectation at your church that members and regular attenders will be part of a small group, and/or a men's or women's group, and/or a mentoring relationship (and is the expectation matched by actual results)?

2. Does your church have a clear, consistent approach for helping visitors and regular attenders to become members, and is the approach regularly adhered to and effective?

3. Does your church intentionally (and perhaps systematically) develop new leaders, with the expectation that they will serve in a key leadership role in the near future?

4. Are the handoffs between children's ministry, middle school ministry, and high school ministry seamless and cohesive, such that there is an easy, natural progression as children age and move from one ministry to the next?

5. Is there a built-in expectation at your church that each Christian not only understand their spiritual gifts but actively

use their gifts in service to Christ and His church (and is the expectation matched by actual results)?

6. As people profess Christ for the first time, are they paired with a spiritual guide or mentor who will walk with them in the early stages of their Christian journey?

7. Does the congregation value connection with one another, regularly sharing meals and spending time together?

8. Does the church place more emphasis on discipleship-based ministry than it does on programs or events?

9. Does the church offer classes/workshops that are designed to help "disciple up" people?

10. Is there a built-in expectation at your church that each Christian is called to share the Gospel in both word and deed with others (and is there evidence of people doing so)?

If you feel discouraged by your answers to the questions above, or for that matter with the unfolding reality of the climate, roots, or soil of your church, know that you are hardly alone. The truth is that most churches struggle in most, or all, of these areas. But what ultimately matters is what we do about what we know to be true.

This section ("Assessment") is important to understand where we are at today, so that we can begin to identify ways to be a more effective church tomorrow. Assessment is not easy work, but it's essential for future health and growth.

QUESTIONS FOR DISCUSSION & REFLECTION

- Describe the current climate at your church.

- In general, are the roots of your leaders, staff, and congregation sufficient to withstand high temperatures?

- What sort of climate change might the church be able to handle in this coming season?

- What soil type/s are present at your church?

- Does the seeding approach at your church reflect a "single-seed" approach, or a "grafting" approach?

6

LEADERSHIP AND STAFF COMMITMENT

There is a direct correlation between success in strategic planning and having a leadership and staff team fully committed to the mission of the church. Prior to beginning a season of planning, take the time to understand and acknowledge where your leadership and staff teams are at, and to make necessary adjustments where possible to foster unity in Christ, and an "all in" commitment to the cause of Christ.

UNITY *IN CHRIST*

A shared unity in Christ is the starting point for staff and leadership health and commitment. Jesus is our common ground. We may disagree on any number of things, but we must be able to agree that Jesus Christ is our Savior and Lord, and the head of His church. Is this enough to resolve every conflict? No, of course not … but it is always the correct starting point.

Make no mistake, the only "unity" that really matters is the unity we share *in Christ*. Unity for the sake of unity is incomplete, and often leads to unholy alliances. In fact, it's not at all uncommon for people on church leadership and staff teams to be united for all the wrong reasons – a common dislike of a staff member or leader, a stance against the current worship style, a clamoring to go back to how things used to be, or opposition to a planning process and all that it entails. The only form of unity that advances the cause of Christ is unity in Christ.

Paul's letter to the Ephesians is a stunning pronouncement of the importance of unity in Christ. Paul wrote to the church in Ephesus to strengthen them in the face of growing opposition, both within and outside the church (some things never change!). Paul immediately set a tone in the letter by using the phrase "*In Christ*," or some variation thereof, no less than ten times in the space of a mere thirteen verses of Ephesians chapter 1:

"The faithful *in Christ Jesus*" (Eph. 1:1)

"Every spiritual blessing *in Christ*" (Eph. 1:3)

"Chose us *in him*" (Eph. 1:4)

"Freely given *in the One he loves*" (Eph. 1:6)

"*In him* we have redemption" (Eph. 1:7)

"Which he purposed *in Christ*" (Eph. 1:9)

"*In him* we were also chosen" (Eph. 1:11)

"The first to hope *in Christ*" (Eph. 1:12)

"Included *in Christ*" (Eph. 1:13a)

"Marked *in him* with a seal" (Eph. 1:13b)

Paul wanted the Ephesian Christians to understand clearly that whatever differences existed among them were insignificant in comparison to the unity they shared in Jesus Christ.

As a pastor, as a leader, are you instilling this same

understanding in your leadership team and staff? Does your team function according to the truth that the One who unites us is more powerful than anything, or anyone, who might try to divide us?

"ALL IN" COMMITMENT

Have you ever had the experience of hearing a person say they're "all in," and then shortly after, when some form of adversity hits, the person is suddenly "all out?" If you've held any sort of leadership role you know exactly what I'm talking about!

Planning requires all hands to be on deck, ready and willing to do what is necessary. Here are eight marks of "all in" leadership and staff teams:

Everyone is praying.
I have yet to see positive results emerge from a season of planning when prayer wasn't at the forefront. Conversely, I have seen amazing success when there is a shared commitment among leaders and staff to be in prayer prior to, during, and after a strategic planning season.

Conversation is marked with grace and truth.
High functioning, fully committed teams emulate Christ by embracing both grace and truth. This allows for hard but necessary discussion to take place without tearing the team apart. Honesty and transparency are essential, but so too is unconditional grace.

There is an earnest desire to grow and improve.
Effective planning requires that we hold a sort of mirror up

to assess where we are at so that we can better understand where God is leading us, and how we might get there. Self-assessment, both personally and corporately, is painful but necessary. The antidote to complacency is to earnestly desire to grow and improve, understanding the past and present while working toward a better future.

Collaboration is the order of the day.
There is no single person who can effectively plan on behalf of an organization. Leadership is needed to be sure, but good leadership is not so much about "doing" as it is about empowering, equipping, and encouraging others to contribute. Collaboration is vital for excelling in formulating and executing plans.

Accountability is understood and embraced.
I have seen planning efforts fizzle as deadlines come and go with seemingly no one noticing. If leadership accountability is lacking, success in planning will be limited at best.

There is genuine excitement around the mission and vision of the church.
While gaining widespread agreement on every plan element is both unlikely and unnecessary, it *is* necessary to have leaders who display genuine passion and enthusiasm for the mission and vision of the church.

There is a willingness to stop ministries, programs, or events that have run their course.

In my experience, stopping ministries, programs, or events is *much* harder than adding ministries, programs, or events. Our common tendency is to add rather than subtract, but the problem is that most churches are already stretched too far. As a general rule, I advise churches and leaders that any ministries or programs they add be offset with ministries or programs that are stopped. Because the guideline is difficult to accept, I introduce it at the onset of the planning process and reinforce it throughout.

Change is expected and embraced.

Let's face it: change is inevitable. The world is constantly changing, and so must we. What worked twenty years ago, or ten years ago, or even last year, might not work this year. Our choice is to change or slowly die. How we view change will largely dictate whether or not we are willing to change, and more to the point, whether we will embrace change as a gift or reject change as a hindrance.

QUESTIONS FOR DISCUSSION & REFLECTION

- Do your leadership and staff teams understand, embrace, and function in accordance with their shared unity *in Christ*?

- How are your leadership and staff teams doing relative to the eight marks listed? (Discuss this question as a team)

- Do you have a Leadership Covenant? Is it effective?

PART THREE

LONG-RANGE PLANNING

If your church has already established its mission, vision, and values, you may be tempted to skip this section and go straight to Annual Planning. But I encourage you not to do so!

Any ability we have to effectively discern and formulate annual plans is contingent on giving ample focus and attention to mission, vision, and values. To skip ahead is to devalue the foundational elements that inform and govern who we are to be, and what we are endeavoring to do.

In the way of an analogy, imagine taking Communion without any express reminder of why we gather around the table, or what the Communion elements represent. Imagine the pastor walking behind the Communion table and declaring, "Since you're all familiar with what took place during Jesus' last supper, there's really no need to rehash all of that now. In fact, we're running a bit late this morning, so let's cut to the chase and do this thing. But as you eat the bread and drink the juice, be sure to ponder the significance of Communion."

Say what?! What pastor would take such a flippant, nonchalant approach to Communion? Granted, most people in our congregations have heard the same words time and time again during Communion, but they're said time and time again because they're incredibly significant.

Yet when it comes to the call that Christ has placed on His church, the call to go and make disciples, our tendency is to say "got it," and shift our focus to more "urgent" matters. But isn't our mission too significant to gloss over? Shouldn't we give our full, undivided attention to the mission call given to us by Christ?

Several years ago I taught Franklin-Covey Time Management. One of the concepts that never failed to resonate with participants is what Covey called the *Time Management Matrix*,[13] shown here:

	URGENT	NOT URGENT
IMPORTANT	I Quadrant of **Necessity**	II Quadrant of **Quality**
UNIMPORTANT	III Quadrant of **Deception**	IV Quadrant of **Waste**

By way of explanation, Quadrant I is the Quadrant of Necessity, in which we spend our time doing things that are both important and urgent. Since life is not meant to be lived in a constant state of crisis, the challenge in Quadrant I is to limit how much time we spend there. Moving down the page, Quadrant III is the Quadrant of Deception, in which we urgently spend time on things that *seem* important but aren't. Here, our challenge is to be discerning, learning to say no to certain requests. To the right, Quadrant IV is the Quadrant of Waste, in which we do things that are neither urgent nor important (think television, video games, social media, etc.). Time spent in Quadrant IV can actually be beneficial as a sort of outlet if (and only if) we impose strict limits on how much time we spend there. Finally, there is Quadrant II, the Quadrant of Quality, in which we spend time on things that are not urgent, but vitally important - prayer, family, relationships, exercise, etc.

The Time Management Matrix has a lesson to teach church leaders. Our common tendency is to do well with limiting our time in Quadrants I and IV, yet failing miserably when it comes to avoiding Quadrant III and investing enough time in Quadrant II.

It seems to me that there are two primary reasons for this problem: lack of clarity, and lack of sacrificial commitment.

When we lack clarity on what we are called to do (mission), and/or what God is leading us to become (vision), and/or the things we hold most dear (values), we process new ideas, requests, and issues through an ever-changing, never-solidifying grid. It's like trying to hit the bullseye on a moving target! A lack of clarity on mission, vision, or values causes us to think that the things we are working on are urgent and important, when oftentimes they're neither. Hence, when we spend excessive time in Quadrant III, it's usually because we haven't spent nearly enough time defining what matters most in Quadrant II.

On the other hand, some pastors and church leaders are clear on their mission, vision, and values, yet nevertheless spend far too much time in Quadrant III. Their challenge is not a lack of clarity, but a lack of *sacrificial* commitment. True sacrifice requires setting aside what we want in favor of what Christ calls and inspires us to do. True sacrifice always costs us something, and oftentimes the price is very, very steep.

Spending time in Quadrant II is critical for pastors and church leaders, but so too is fully committing to set aside what we want in favor of what Christ asks of us. The mission we have been given is worth sacrificing for. In fact, it's worth giving everything for.

7

MISSION

If you clamor for a hearty debate, invite a group of pastors and church leaders in for a discussion on mission and vision. One side of the room will insist that vision is what matters most - that identifying and committing to a white hot vision is ultimately how the church stops wandering and begins to bear fruit. The other side of the room will insist that mission is what matters most - that having a clear, concise mission is what drives a church to become fruitful. As the conversation ensues, it will become increasingly apparent that the room is split on what constitutes, and differentiates, mission and vision. And you might hear conversations like this:

PASTOR A: "The mission of our church is to impact our community, nation, and world for Jesus Christ. We have identified a lot of ways to do that - school partnerships, a food ministry, programs for kids, missionary partnerships."

PASTOR B: "At our church, we consider our mission to be making disciples, since that's the mission given to us by Christ."

PASTOR A: "Yes, of course! But being a disciple-making church is a vision, not a mission. It's a vision because it's always set before us, and you can never fully 'arrive' because there's always more people to reach. So the way we see it, if we do the right things - if we impact our community for Christ - we're being faithful to the mission while stepping toward the vision."

PASTOR B: "I understand your point, and I think we're kind of saying the same thing, but our paradigm of mission and vision is opposite of yours. We agree that you never fully arrive at being a disciple-making church, and that's exactly why we see it as our mission, as the reason we exist as a church. Our mission is always before us, and we can never check the box and call it complete. But a vision *can* be realized, which is why vision can change from time to time."

And so goes the mission and vision conversation! By now, you probably have a good idea of my viewpoint on the mission-vision debate, which is to side with Pastor B. But the reason I feel strongly that mission must always come before, and be held above, vision, wasn't expressed in the imaginary dialogue above.

What is the basis for my position? Simply that whereas the vision of a church is discerned by people, the mission of a church – to go and make disciples - is a *command* from Christ. To be sure, if approached in a manner befitting the task, vision will be inspired by the Holy Spirit. But ultimately vision is discerned by a person, or a group of people. Mission, though, is God given, and must always come before, and be held above, vision.

STAYING "ON MISSION": LESSONS FROM THE SEVEN CHURCHES IN REVELATION

We've already touched on the importance of staying "on mission," and the challenge that doing so represents in light of our tendency to wander. But I'd like to go deeper on this topic by examining what Jesus spoke to the seven churches in Revelation. Jesus' words have much to teach us about the importance of staying on mission, how churches drift from mission, the consequences of drifting from mission, and the opportunities Christ provides to repent and start afresh.

For proper context, it is important to recall that the seven churches addressed in Revelation were actual churches at the time John wrote Revelation. Though none of these churches exists today, each is emblematic of modern day churches. Their lessons are our lessons.

On that note, I invite you to step away for a few minutes to read Revelation 2 and 3.

∞∞∞∞

One thing that emerges rather clearly in these two chapters is the consistent, patterned approach in which Jesus addresses the churches. Typically, Jesus commends the church for what they are doing well, rebukes the church for how they have drifted, warns the church of the consequences of failing to repent, and gives the church an opportunity to repent and start afresh with a clean slate.

This pattern – commendation, rebuke, warning, and opportunity - presents itself in totality at three of the seven churches: Ephesus, Pergamum, and Thyatira. But when Jesus addresses Smyrna and Philadelphia, there is only commendation and opportunity, for in those churches there is nothing to rebuke or warn against. And when Jesus addresses Sardis and Laodicea, there is no commendation, though amazingly both are offered opportunities to repent and be restored.

As you read ahead, take time to consider what Jesus might speak to your church in light of what He spoke to the churches in Revelation. What might you learn from those who have gone before us? How might the Spirit speak to you?

> "Whoever has ears, let them hear what the Spirit says to the churches." (Rev. 2:7, 2:11, 2:17, 2:29, 3:6, 3:13, 3:22)

Ephesus

Jesus commends the church in Ephesus for their good deeds (2:2), hard work (2:2), perseverance (2:2), discernment (2:2), commitment (2:3), and intolerance of false Christianity (2:6). However, Jesus rebukes the church for allowing their love of Christ to diminish (2:4), and warns them that if they fail to repent, they will lose favor with Christ (2:5). Finally, Jesus presents the church with three intertwined opportunities: To take stock of where they are and how far they have fallen (2:5); to repent and get back to where they were (2:5); and to listen for and follow the Holy Spirit (2:7).

What we learn from Ephesus, and for that matter from each of the seven churches in Revelation, is not easily summarized. In fact, if you heed the seven-fold invitation to "Hear what the Spirit says to the churches," it is likely that you will come away with additional learnings beyond what I list, along with a sense of how those learnings apply to you individually and to your church as a whole. Hence, what is presented here is strictly a starting point - it's up to you to seek the Spirit's leading to go beyond.

A church that has cooled in its passion and fervor for Christ and His Gospel can (and often does) continue doing the right things: good deeds, hard work, perseverance, commitment. But if our "doing" is increasingly disconnected from our "being" (who we are in Christ), and if our focus shifts to what needs to be done rather than the One in whose name we do it, our love for Christ will diminish. Many churches do a multitude of good things, and many are filled with people who know their bibles well but have cooled in their love for Christ and people.

Do you see this happening in your church? Has religion been elevated to a higher place than relationship? Listen to what the Spirit is saying.

Churches that have lost the deep love for Christ they once held must repent and start afresh. In essence, Jesus calls the church in Ephesus to go all the way back to the beginning, when they were a church on fire, a church burning with love for Christ and people. It's especially noteworthy that Jesus doesn't call the church to stop what they are doing, but to change their motivation - to "do the things you did at first," not out of habit or obligation, but out of love.

The church in Ephesus did good things yet drifted in their love for Christ. The same can be said of many modern day Christians, and churches. If that's the case for you personally, or for your church in general, repent and go back. You need not stop what you are doing, but you must fall in love afresh with Christ and His church. The only way that we can truly be successful in our mission to "go and make disciples" is to do so in conjunction with loving God, and loving people, with all that we have – heart, mind, soul, and strength. The Great Commission and Great Commandment are inextricably linked. You simply cannot have one without the other.

Smyrna

Jesus commends the church in Smyrna for their spiritual vibrancy in the face of hardship and poverty (2:9). Jesus issues no rebuke or warning, but informs them that for a brief time they will suffer for the cause of Christ (2:10) and then, should they remain faithful, receive the victor's crown (2:10). Finally, Jesus exhorts them to listen for and follow the Holy Spirit (2:11).

What Jesus speaks to the church in Smyrna ought to encourage any church that faces hardship, yet remains faithful and vibrant!

Jesus acknowledges the daily challenges that impoverished churches face, yet makes clear that what these churches lack materially, they receive in abundance spiritually. As always, the words of Jesus run counter to what the world values, and if we're honest about it, what many in western Christendom value. Far too many churches, and far too many church leaders, are forever clamoring for more – more people, more finances, more building space, more programs, more volunteers, more of this and more of that – yet discount the spiritual value in being content with, and thankful for, what they have.

Practically speaking, the problem with always clamoring for more is that we never fully optimize, or even utilize, the resources we already have. Invariably, dwelling on what we don't have results in a failure to use what we do have.

Is your church like Smyrna? Are you mired in poverty, lacking resources? If so, count it as a blessing! It is easier for you to cling to the truth that God provides all that is needed for the call He has given you. Like Smyrna, if you are able to remain vibrant and faithful to your mission, even in the face of duress and poverty, you will be blessed with spiritual riches.

Christ tells the church in Smyrna that He knows about "the slander of those who say they are Jews and are not, but are a synagogue of Satan." In essence, Jesus is telling them that He understands the difficulty in dealing with religious people who claim to know God, yet are far from God. Christ commends the church in Smyrna for remaining faithful while rebuking misguided people who would cause the church to drift off mission if they were allowed to gain a foothold in the church.

Do you find yourself dealing with religious people who claim to be godly yet are anything but? If so, be diligent to not allow self-righteous people to hold positions of influence in the church. Guard your hearts, and guard the mission call of Christ, by remaining faithful to Christ during all circumstances. Rest assured that Jesus knows your struggle, and will reward your faith with the victor's crown.

Pergamum

Jesus commends the church in Pergamum for continuing to proclaim the Gospel in spite of the rampant evil and corruption around them (2:13). However, Jesus rebukes the church for allowing false teaching and evil practices to exist in the church (2:14-15). Jesus warns Pergamum that if they fail to repent, He will pour out His wrath upon those who have steered the church astray (2:16), but if they do repent, they will be *eternally* adopted as unique, beloved children of the King (2:17). Jesus concludes by inviting the church to listen for and follow the Holy Spirit (2:17).

Jesus recognizes the unique challenge of being His witnesses in places where evil abounds. Pergamum was a pagan city, a place with temples for Greek and Roman gods, and for the people to worship the Roman Emperor. The church in Pergamum was heavily persecuted, as are many churches today. In fact, according to Open Doors, 2014 saw more global persecution of Christians than any other year in recent history.[14] Yet paradoxically, in the economy of God, persecuted churches often flourish. The advance of the Gospel cannot be stopped.

It is telling that of the top twenty countries where Christianity is growing the fastest, twelve of them - China, United Arab Emirates, Saudi Arabia, Qatar, Oman, Yemen, Bahrain, South Sudan, Bhutan, Mali, Brunei, and Kuwait - are also on the 2014 world watch list of the top fifty countries where Christians face the greatest persecution.[15] Jesus' promise to the church in Pergamum of "hidden manna" and "a white stone with a new name written on it" make clear that our Lord holds a special place for those who endure persecution and emerge victorious.

Does your church face persecution? If so, be encouraged by what Jesus speaks to Pergamum, for those words are for you as well. Conversely, if your church is relatively free of persecution, consider how the Holy Spirit might be leading you to walk beside and support those that do. Taking stock of our mission to "go and make disciples" should prompt us to consider ways that we can strengthen other churches, especially those that are persecuted.

Even as Jesus commends the church in Pergamum for proclaiming the Gospel in an environment of hostility, He rebukes them for allowing false teaching and evil practices to infiltrate the church.

How does a church so committed to the Gospel, so faithful in proclaiming Christ in the face of horrific persecution, allow false teaching and evil practices to enter the church? Most often, it happens gradually, imperceptibly, like bad yeast working slowly yet steadily through a batch of dough.

Notice that when Jesus rebukes the church in Pergamum, He begins by saying, "There are some *among you.*" Pergamum, a church commended for staying strong for Christ in the face of outside persecution, was led astray from within. The leaders of the church were so focused on protecting the flock against outside corruption that they allowed internal corruption to gain a foothold.

We must be vigilant to watch out for false prophets, those who wear sheep's clothing but inwardly are ferocious wolves (Matthew 7:15). Just as attending a church does not in itself bring salvation, neither does being a member of a church qualify a person for leadership.

The rebuke Jesus issued to the church in Pergamum had more to do with leadership negligence than leadership abdication. And while negligence may seem more palatable than abdication, it should never be held up as an excuse. Pergamum is a prime example of what leadership negligence leads to, and that the antidote for negligence is vigilance.

How are you doing at ensuring that what is preached and taught at your church aligns with the truth of Scripture? Are you selective when it comes to who leads? Do you hold leaders accountable at all times? Is keeping the church "on mission" a higher priority than trying to keep people happy? Listen to what the Spirit is saying.

Thyatira

Jesus commends the church in Thyatira for their charity (2:19), love (2:19), faith (2:19), service (2:19), perseverance (2:19), and spiritual growth (2:19). Jesus rebukes the church for tolerating a person who has blatantly led others in the church to commit evil acts (2:20). Jesus warns them that those who inflict evil, or allow evil, will experience His wrath (2:22). Finally, Jesus gives the church several opportunities: To not stray, so that no additional burdens will be imposed (2:24); to "hold on," for Jesus is coming soon (2:25); to do God's will, so that they receive authority (2:26-27) and wisdom (2:28); and to listen for and follow the Holy Spirit (2:29).

Before Jesus rebukes the church in Thyatira, He commends them for "doing more" than they did at first. Evidently, the church was experiencing spiritual growth, a season in which what they did was properly aligned with who they were in Christ. But even as they were growing spiritually, they were allowing evil to gain a foothold in the church. At a cursory glance, the issues in Thyatira seem remarkably similar to the issues in Pergamum: false teaching, idolatry, and sexual immorality. But a closer look reveals that while the issues were similar, how they got there was quite different.

Whereas Pergamum was unduly influenced by a group of people from within the church, Thyatira was held sway by a person outside of the church. And whereas the evil practices that took root in Pergamum likely developed slowly and subtly, the evil practices that took root in Thyatira came quickly and unmistakably. Finally, whereas the root issue in Pergamum was leadership negligence, the root issue in Thyatira was leadership tolerance. The results were essentially the same at both churches, but how they arrived there was markedly different.

It is telling that Jesus begins His rebuke of Thyatira by saying, "You *tolerate* that woman Jezebel, who calls herself a prophet."

80

While the person's name likely wasn't Jezebel, Jesus' reference to "Jezebel" indicates that this individual needed to be dealt with sternly. Yet the root issue isn't that "Jezebel" was seeking to steer the Christians in Thyatira toward evil, but that the church leaders in Thyatira allowed her to do so; that they *tolerated* her.

To understand the severity of what this person was allowed to bring to the church in Thyatira, we need to recall the wickedness of the original Jezebel in the Old Testament, who was bent on mingling worship of Baal with worship of God. But unlike the original Jezebel, this Jezebel goes one step further by claiming to be a prophet, though clearly she was not.

All of this begs a fundamental question: *How could the leaders at Thyatira tolerate a person so clearly bent on evil?*

Well … imagine a person walks into your church and says, "God told me that our mission to 'go and make disciples' is to be changed to 'go and make friends.' God explained to me that because Jesus calls us 'friends,' and because in our culture the word 'friend' is less offensive than 'disciple,' we need to change our mission accordingly."

What would your response be? Most of us, I think, would react with mild amusement and a gentle rebuke, thanking the person for stopping in but explaining that our mission call will remain intact, thank you very much.

But suppose this person begins to share his belief with other people in the church. Suppose that the person begins to seek out people who lack the spiritual maturity to properly discern that making 'friends' is not nearly the same as making 'disciples.' Suppose that more and more people begin to come around to his way of thinking, believing that since God "told" him it must be so. Now what do you do? Do you ignore the situation, believing it to be a harmless blip on the radar brought on by one misguided person? Or do you address the person with firmness and specificity, explaining that the church will not tolerate teaching that goes against scripture?

The church in Thyatira chose to overlook – to tolerate – Jezebel, and in doing so allowed evil, detestable practices to permeate the church. They likely believed that what one misguided person was spreading couldn't possibly gain a foothold in a faith community that was growing spiritually, doing more than they did at first. Their toleration of this person amounted to leadership abdication, which paved the way for blatant sin to permeate and spoil the church.

As pastors and leaders, we must extend grace, giving people ample opportunity to repent and be restored. That is, after all, what Jesus did with Jezebel of Thyatira: "I have given her time to repent of her immorality, but she is unwilling" (Rev. 2:21). But truth must always accompany grace, and if it doesn't, grace will inevitably yield to tolerance.

One final lesson from Thyatira: While the leaders abdicated their responsibility, there were many in the church who stood firm in the truth of Jesus Christ, and refused to succumb to the corruption around them. Jesus' encouragement to "hold on" until He comes is for them, and for all who remain committed to the Gospel in spite of being surrounded with false teaching and detestable practices.

Sardis

The church in Sardis receives no commendation from Jesus. Rather, Jesus rebukes the church for appearing to be alive, yet in reality being lifeless (3:1). Further, Jesus doesn't so much warn Sardis as inform them that contrary to their healthy appearance, they are sick and will soon die, ceasing to exist as a church (3:2). Nevertheless, Jesus encourages the church to finish well by repenting so that they might "wake up" and hold fast to the freedom they received through Christ, which they had initially embraced (3:2-3). And Jesus acknowledges that there are a few people in Sardis who have remained righteous, and will be counted worthy (3:4-5). In closing, Jesus encourages Sardis – and all churches - to listen for and follow the Holy Spirit (3:6).

Given that Sardis was a city known for wealth and materialism, it is no surprise that the church in Sardis followed suit. Like the city itself, the church appeared to be vibrant and full of life, though in reality it was anything but. And it is probably fair to say that much of the problem in Sardis stemmed from not having to deal with any problems.

The church in Sardis reminds us that while people look at outward appearances, God looks at what lies within (1 Sam. 16:7). Sardis had a sterling reputation as a church brimming with life, but Christ knew that their outward appearance did not match their spiritual condition. And Christ knew that the church was already dead, having long forgotten the Gospel that they had received from the beginning.

Is your church one that appears vibrant and energetic, yet is inwardly wasting away? If so, you are hardly alone. There are many churches like Sardis - churches filled with programs, activities, and events, but not disciples.

From the outside in, it's easy to admire churches that offer abundant programs and activities; churches that are constantly growing, that seem to be immune from financial hardship or persecution. Who wouldn't want to be part of a church like that?! But activity does not equate to vibrancy, numerical growth does not equate to spiritual growth, and prosperity does not equate to purpose. Our mission is to make disciples, not programs.

It is telling that Jesus does not encourage the church in Sardis to repent so that they can start over, but that they might finish well. Perhaps the reason lies in the fact that whereas Pergamum and Thyatira were marked by a large majority remaining faithful and committed, Sardis was marked by just "a few people" who did so. Jesus knew that the church in Sardis was ready to die, yet He still encouraged the church to repent, holding fast to what they had received.

Philadelphia

Jesus commends the church in Philadelphia for persevering (3:8), remaining faithful (3:8), and enduring patiently (3:10). Jesus does not rebuke or warn the church, but encourages them by promising evangelistic opportunities (3:8), keeping them safe from those who stand against them (3:9), shielding them during a time of global strife (3:10), and exhorting them to "hold on" to the crown they have already received, with the assurance that Christ is coming soon (3:11). Jesus concludes by promising the church in Philadelphia eternal communion with God (3:12), and by exhorting them to listen for and follow the Holy Spirit (3:13).

What an amazing church! The Greek word *Philadelphia* means "brotherly love," and the church in Philadelphia certainly lived up to its name. Jesus' commendation of the church in Philadelphia is astounding. They are a model church, one we are wise to emulate.

What made the church in Philadelphia so extraordinary? First and foremost, the church was unwavering in its faith and reliance on God. Jesus commends Philadelphia for having "little strength" while keeping His word and proclaiming His Gospel. Essentially, Jesus affirms Philadelphia for embracing the truth that their strength lies not in what they are able to do, but in what God does in and through them. Indeed, God rewarded their faith by converting their human weakness into divine strength, so much so that those who would oppose the church would eventually recognize God's favor upon the church, and fall on their knees in response. This was a church that was completely, unabashedly sold out to Christ.

What would happen if churches would heed the example set by the church in Philadelphia? What would happen if church leaders set aside their own dreams and agendas in favor of absolute reliance on God's promises, provision, and leading?

More than anything, the church would function as Christ designed it to function. It is possible that we would have less buildings, less programs, and less people, but it is certain that God would provide more opportunities – more *open doors* – to share the Gospel in word and deed.

On that note, Jesus' words to Philadelphia reinforce the truth that He alone opens (and closes) doors, which we are invited to walk through in order to advance the Gospel. Our responsibility is simply to open our eyes to how God is working in and around us, and to cooperate fully with what God is already doing.

This serves as a good reminder that while strategic planning in the marketplace is focused on taking control in order to bring about a specific result, strategic planning in the church is focused on releasing control, trusting that God will bring the increase, as only God can.

Laodicea

The church in Laodicea receives no commendation from Jesus. Rather, Jesus rebukes Laodicea for being lukewarm (3:16), and for failing to realize their own depravity (3:17). Jesus warns the church that He is close to expelling them (3:16), yet gives them an opportunity to repent and receive discipline (3:18-19), and to be in communion with Christ (3:20). Finally, Jesus exhorts them – and us - to listen for and follow the Holy Spirit (3:22).

In the summer of 2010 I went on a mission trip to Cap-Haïtien, Haiti. The charter of our team was to repair faulty water pumps in select villages, bringing clean water to people in the name of Jesus. Interestingly, even as we helped to provide clean water to others, we ourselves drank from large jugs of water brought from other clean water sources (as westerners, we would be incapable of quickly adapting to the water we were providing, which while clean was less clean than what we were accustomed to). The water we drank was healthy enough, but it was also lukewarm, and took some getting used to.

Having endured a week of drinking lukewarm water in smoldering conditions, I was delighted to consume massive amounts of both cold and hot beverages upon my return. I had no desire to drink even one more lukewarm beverage!

There is little good to be said about being lukewarm in any sense, and absolutely nothing good about being spiritually lukewarm. The church in Laodicea, being neither hot nor cold, surely deserved the rebuke they received from Christ.

Jesus commands His followers to love God with *all* of our heart, *all* of our soul, and *all* of our mind, and to love other people as we ourselves want to be loved. This kind of love, both for God and others, is *not* lukewarm or cold, but red hot.

But Jesus' words to Laodicea make clear that outside of burning love, He would much prefer that we be cold, perhaps even opposed to the things of God, rather than lukewarm. Why? Because people who are spiritually empty, far from God, are much more likely to realize their emptiness than are partially filled, religious people. It is telling that Jesus reached prostitutes and tax collectors, people far from God, but not religious leaders, who claimed to know God.

The church in Laodicea believed itself to be rich, not because of what God gave them, but because they had "acquired wealth" all on their own. Laodicea was marked by arrogance and self-sufficiency, which in combination made them lukewarm – indifferent – toward Christ. But Jesus words to Laodicea make clear that those who are spiritually lukewarm are blind to their true condition, which in the case of Laodicea was "wretched, pitiful, poor, blind, and naked."

The rebuke Jesus gives Laodicea is one that we had better pay attention to. If your church begins to believe that it has "acquired" what God has allowed the church to steward for His glory, you are in trouble; if your leaders place more trust in themselves than in God, you're in trouble; if your church places more value on protocol than making disciples, you're in trouble. Still, amazingly, Jesus remains gracious, standing at the door and knocking. Now it's our move.

"Whoever has ears, let them hear what the Spirit says to the churches." (Rev. 2:7, 2:11, 2:17, 2:29, 3:6, 3:13, 3:22)

MISSION "ON PURPOSE"

By now you know where I stand on the importance of fully committing to mission, and that every church's mission is the Great Commission, undergirded by the Great Commandment.

It ought to be easy to craft a mission statement that encapsulates the Great Commission, but there are many pastors and church leaders who are consumed with developing a mission statement that is somehow more captivating, unique, cutting edge, than the mission Christ gave us. The result is that too many churches have mission statements that relegate the Great Commission to an afterthought.

How does this happen? Why does this happen? Usually, for one of three reasons:

Competing interests.

The demands on pastors, staff members, and lay leaders to do this and try that are never ending. Hardly a day passes without being exposed to some new program, idea, or opportunity. But the risk of constantly trying new things, or forever searching for the next big thing, is that we forget why we exist as a church. Michael Horton addresses this in his book, *Ordinary*:

"Radical. Epic. Revolutionary. Transformative. Impactful. Life-Changing. Ultimate. Extreme. Awesome. Emergent. Alternative. Innovative. On the Edge. The Next Big Thing. The Explosive Breakthrough. You can probably add to the list of modifiers that become, ironically, part of the ordinary conversations in society in today's church."[16]

Horton points out how the church has mirrored the culture in opting for sensationalism over substance. But isn't the Great Commission in itself radical? Epic? Revolutionary?

Confusion between mission and vision.
As already mentioned, there is much confusion in church leadership as to what constitutes, and differentiates, mission and vision. Oftentimes the result is that the time and energy spent on discerning "mission" is actually (and unknowingly) spent on discerning vision.

Equating purpose with mission.
I believe this to be most prevalent of the three reasons listed, and for good reason. Rick Warren's landmark book, *The Purpose-Driven Church*, challenged pastors and church leaders to make purpose their first priority, and to have all that we do be driven by the essential purposes of the church. Through solid exegesis, Warren identified five core purposes of the church: worship, ministry (service), evangelism, fellowship, and discipleship. [17]

Many churches, including those that I have served directly, have adopted these purposes, which help immensely to focus on what matters most. However, some churches have taken the additional step of defining their mission as the five purposes. I believe this misses the mark, albeit just slightly.

The five purposes are essential for church functionality, but they do not, individually or in combination, articulate the mission of the church; why we exist as a church. The purposes are vital for bringing forth mission, but do not represent the mission itself. Rather, they represent a *means* of bringing the mission to fruition.

QUESTIONS FOR DISCUSSION & REFLECTION

- Which church in Revelation do you most identify with? Why?

- Have you experienced "mission drift" at any point in your ministry? If so, what steps did you take to come back to the mission?

- Why is staying "on mission" so difficult?

- In what ways do the purposes of a church serve to bring forth mission?

8

VISION

"GO WEST": A VISION TALE

It was time. Josh knew it. So did Lauren. But it wouldn't be easy. The Wests lived paycheck to paycheck, making ends meet but with little left to spare. For Josh and Lauren, the thought of a family vacation seemed like a distant dream, far beyond their grasp. At least until a few hours ago.

It started innocently enough. The Wests gathered around the table for their usual Saturday breakfast. Josh prayed, eggs and bacon were plated, and it was time to dig in. Josh, Lauren, and 6-year old Malachi (Kai) wasted no time. But 8-year old Iris grabbed her fork, and just as quickly set it back down. A few seconds later came the question: "Mom, dad, do you think we could ever go on a vacation? Kelly keeps talking about her trip to Disney World, and I know we could never go there, but do you think we'll ever go on *any* vacation?"

Josh and Lauren looked at one another, each waiting for the other to respond. Finally, Lauren found the words. "Sweetie, I would love for us to go on vacation, but I'm just not sure we can afford it. But, then again, dad did get a raise last year, and I've picked up a few more hours. Hmmm … how about if dad and I talk about it and let you guys know, okay?"

Iris nodded excitedly and began to eat. Kai bellowed, "cool!" Josh nodded in silence.

Later that morning, after the children went outside to play, Lauren asked Josh if he was upset with her. Josh assured her that he was more nervous than upset. But the more they talked, the more they agreed that it was time - past time, really – for a family vacation.

Thirty minutes later anxiety gave way to excitement. They began to dream about a vacation that would bring them closer as a family; a vacation that each would cherish for years. And so they came up with a plan. Well, not really a plan. More like a plan that would help them to create a plan.

Nine hours later, the pizza arrived, signaling the start of dinner and the unveiling of the plan that would help create *the plan*. After a few bites, Josh began: "Well, this morning Iris brought up the idea of a family vacation. Mom and I have talked about it, and we think Iris is right, that we should go away for a family vacation. So Iris, Kai – what do you guys think?"

Iris bellowed a hearty "yessss," while Kai began to run in circles, high fiving his sister, mother, and father. Josh and Lauren looked at each other and smiled, then Lauren gave Josh the nod to continue. "Well, I guess we're going on vacation then. But there is one little catch. Mom and I figured out how we can save around $200 each month, but to do it we'll need to make some sacrifices. We'll need to drop the premium movie channels from our cable package, only go out to dinner once a month, and start buying more generic brand groceries. And we're going to have a garage sale this spring, which we expect you both to help with. Last thing - no more hot lunches at school for a while. You'll both have to start taking a lunch from home. Now, if you're both agreeable to all of that, we can go on a family vacation. So how about it?"

Iris and Kai nodded their approval, though not until Kai was sufficiently comfortable that "generic" groceries weren't the same as "germed" groceries.

Iris looked ready to say something, but Josh spoke first. "One other thing. Mom and I want us to work together as a family to figure out where we're going and when we're going, and for that matter how we're going to get there. Now, if we save $200 each month, we would have around $2,400 in a year. We did some research, and for us to go to Disney World for a week and really do it right, the total cost would be close to $5,000. So it would take us around two years before we could go to Disney. Or, if we wanted to do something sooner, we could go somewhere else this summer, and save up for Disney over the next few years. So, Iris, Kai, what do you guys think we should do?"

"Two years until Disney! That's like forever!" said an exasperated Kai.

Iris, looking equally troubled, chimed in. "Two years is a long time to wait. But Disney would be so cool! I guess ... I guess I want to go *somewhere* this summer, but still go to Disney some other time." Kai nodded in agreement.

"Well guys, it turns out that mom and I were thinking along the same lines," replied Josh. "How about this. We found a vacation planning website that has a checklist. Since we know that we want to go somewhere this summer, why don't we start working through it now?"

Lauren was way ahead of him. She placed the checklist on the table for all to see. "This says we should start by asking everyone in the family what their hopes and expectations are for the vacation. Then it says we should determine where we want to go and how we will travel – plane, train, car, whatever. Then it's on to lodging, meals, entertainment and activities. Now, there's a bunch of other stuff in here too, but this is where they say you should start. So … who wants to go first? Who wants to talk about what you hope for on this vacation?"

Kai instinctively raised his hand. "Umm, I would like to go somewhere cool that has rides. And ice cream. Lots of ice cream. And rides. And souvenirs. Oh, and a swimming pool. With rides."

Iris rolled her eyes and weighed in. "I think that we should go somewhere fun, and rides are cool, but princesses are way better than rides, and Kelly says that all the princesses live at Disney. But, yeah, some place that has rides would be fun. Like maybe one of those huge amusement parks that kids at school talk about all the time."

Josh nodded and looked at Lauren. "What about you? What would you want for our vacation?" Lauren paused for a moment, then began. "I think more than anything I would want us to do a lot of things together as a family. Rides are fun, so are princesses - and Iris you *are* a princess - but I really just want for us to be together and make great memories. Oh, and I would love to have at least one day to go to a beach."

Finally, it was Josh's turn. "Well, like mom, more than anything I want us to enjoy our time together – to have fun and make memories. So how about this: Instead of going to one place, what if we went to a bunch of places? What if instead of staying at a resort, we went on a road trip out west? Like through Colorado, and maybe Wyoming and Arizona? I remember Uncle Roy saying a few years ago that if we ever wanted to borrow their camper they would be happy to let us use it. We could have an adventure vacation, where we make plans as we go along. But I promise, we would find a cool amusement park along the way, and a beach too."

Kai excitedly weighed in. "Would it be like a pirate adventure? You know, like would we be pirates who sail the seas, except in a camper? That would be awesome!"

Before Josh could answer, Iris said, "No Kai, dad didn't say we would be pirates. We would be, like, adventurers, or explorers, or whatever that word is. But not pirates!"

Kai sighed. "Well, it would still be cool. And I am going to be a pirate, not an adventure guy."

Lauren smiled. "Kai, you can be a pirate, and Iris, you can be an explorer – an explorer princess. I think this is going to be one amazing vacation! So, are we all in?"

LESSONS FROM THE WEST FAMILY

The West family has much to teach us about vision! In no particular order, here are some lessons we can glean from this imaginary tale …

Vision is borne of discontent

Iris West was upset, and when she shared what was bothering her, it led to major changes for her family. In *Holy Discontent*, Bill Hybels makes the case that when a person is discontent over a matter that also brings discontent to God, the person's discontentment is holy – righteous – and instrumental for bringing forth a personal vision that is also holy. [18] Of course, the opposite is true as well - that if we are discontent over matters that bother us but do not bother God, than any vision springing from our discontent will be unholy.

But there is another, often overlooked dynamic that we must recognize - that one person's (or group's) unholy discontent can effectively spur others in proximity to enter into a season of deep, honest reflection of what is and what should be. And it's in seasons of deep and honest reflection that clarity often emerges about what to *legitimately* be discontented about, and how to make right what is clearly wrong.

Iris West's discontentment was borne not of holiness, but envy. Still, it prompted her parents to take stock of where they were at as a family, and to begin formulating a vision that would bring them closer together than ever before. And while the Wests are a fictional family in a fictional tale, this dynamic – unholy discontent in one person or group followed by honest reflection and increased clarity by another person or group – does in fact play out in living rooms, boardrooms, and churches on a daily basis. The key for church leaders is to pray and process for however long it takes in order to gain clarity on what grieves both ourselves and God, for it's in that place where *holy* discontent is found, and a holy vision begins to emerge.

Sacrifice always accompanies vision

Josh and Lauren West moved from anxiety to excitement when they allowed themselves to dream. Yet even as they began to envision a vacation that would bring their family closer together while producing lifelong memories, they were careful to count the cost. Josh and Lauren determined that by making some small sacrifices, they could save around $200 each month toward their vacation. They added to their wisdom by enfolding their children, inviting each to determine whether the sacrifices necessary to go on vacation were worth making. The result was that the family entered into a sort of covenant, in which together they would embark on a season of shared sacrifice in order to realize a vision that just hours before didn't exist.

Unfortunately, the wisdom shown by the Wests eludes many churches. Far too often, leaders discern and cast a vision but fail to project and communicate the cost of the vision, and the need for church members to sacrifice in order to realize the vision.

And to be clear, "cost" goes well beyond finances. If the vision of a church includes building a new worship center, it is both easy and normative to communicate the estimated financial cost prior to initiating a pledge drive. But if the same vision necessitates a change in worship style, the cost – the *sacrifice* - will have increased substantially for some members. And if the vision also entails enfolding people with developmental disability, the cost will have risen still more for members who are concerned that chaos will replace the order they've been accustomed to.

The adage that "one change changes everything" rings true for all organizations. But for churches, where comfort tends to be the order of the day, it is especially prevalent. A holy and compelling vision does not guarantee that congregants, or for that matter pastors and leaders, will be willing to sufficiently sacrifice in order for the vision to come to fruition.

The counterpart to counting the cost is to count the "loss" – to consider the consequences of knowing what we ought to do, but failing to do it. Other than Christ Himself, perhaps the best illustration of what it means to count both cost and loss, and to sacrifice everything in support of a worthwhile vision, is Dr.

Martin Luther King, Jr.   King knew that many people wanted him dead, but he determined that he would pay whatever price was necessary to carry out the holy vision he held dear. Dr. King's vision was expressed many times in many places, most notably on August 28, 1963 on the steps of the Lincoln Memorial:

> "I have a dream that one day this nation will rise up and live out the true meaning of its creed: 'We hold these truths to be self-evident; that all men are created equal.' I have a dream that one day on the red hills of Georgia the sons of former slaves and the sons of former slave owners will be able to sit down together at the table of brotherhood. I have a dream that one day even the state of Mississippi, a state sweltering with the heat of injustice, sweltering with the heat of oppression, will be transformed into an oasis of freedom and justice. I have a dream that my four little children will one day live in a nation where they will not be judged by the color of their skin but by the content of their character. I have a dream today. I have a dream that one day down in Alabama, with its vicious racists, with its governor having his lips dripping with the words of interposition and nullification, that one day right down in Alabama little black boys and black girls will be able to join hands with little white boys and white girls as sisters and brothers. I have a dream that one day every valley shall be exalted, every hill and mountain shall be made low, the rough places will be made plain, and the crooked places will be made straight, and the glory of the Lord shall be revealed, and all flesh shall see it together."[19]

Vision requires honest, courageous leadership

Lauren West's initial response to her daughter's lament was telling: "I would love for us to go on vacation, but I'm just not sure we can afford it." Lauren in effect admitted that neither she nor Josh had ever considered how they might save money for a vacation, only that they were "just not sure" that it was feasible. Isn't this the same thing that happens in churches? Someone – a pastor, a staff member, a lay leader, a congregant – will suggest a change, and the response back is, "I'm just not sure," which tends to be code for, "Thanks for your idea. Let's target implementation on the twelfth – of never!"

But Lauren's response to Iris didn't stop with "just not sure." Instead, she paused to consider recent developments – Josh's raise, her extra hours – and committed to considering Iris's question more carefully in consultation with Josh. Lauren took the less traveled path of leadership rather than the overcrowded road of convenience. And in short order, Josh joined Lauren on the leadership pathway.

The interaction between Lauren and Josh is both instructive and emblematic of true leaders. The respect they hold for each other is apparent in many ways – giving one another ample space to think and speak, affirming one another in front of the children, checking with one another to gauge if there is conflict to work through, and communicating to their children in a manner both unified (one message) and invitational (encouraging their children to enter into the conversation).

More than that, both Josh and Lauren lead out of who they truly are. Their personalities emerge through their interactions, and each is comfortable leading from their true self. Lauren openly expresses her concern regarding affordability, yet quickly follows with a commitment to explore possible options with Josh. She demonstrates leadership that is both honest and courageous. Josh is even more nervous than Lauren, but chooses to reveal his anxiety in private with Lauren, rather than when the children are present. In doing so, Josh reinforces a key leadership principle: That while transparency is a necessary attribute for leaders, wise leaders are selective about what they reveal, and to whom they reveal it. And Josh, like Lauren, exemplifies courageous leadership, setting aside anxiety in favor of dreaming about what could be, and taking some simple steps to allow their dream to become reality.

Josh and Lauren are emblematic of pastors and church leaders insofar as they are not immune against insecurity, doubt, and reactionary leadership. Their struggles are our struggles. But I pray that their decision to not stay stuck in place, but to lead with unity, honesty and courage, is our decision as well.

The notion that vision must always be discerned by the senior leader is a myth

Many pastors and church leaders hold the mistaken belief that it is the sole responsibility of the lead pastor to discern a church's vision. This belief puts inordinate and misplaced pressure on a single person, and restricts other leaders from fully stepping into their call to lead.

In the case of the Wests, their vision was not so much discerned by a person as by a group, with each person playing a different but pivotal role. Iris planted the seed when she expressed her discontent; Lauren stepped out in faith by committing that she and Josh would consider Iris's question further; Josh set aside personal anxiety in order to dream about, and then begin to plan for, what might be possible; and Kai, with the others, helped shape and refine the vision.

To be clear, I am not suggesting that all members of a church (or for that matter a staff or leadership board) must agree on a vision before proceeding accordingly. Nor am I suggesting that church members should actively participate in the task of discerning vision. The first scenario would result in organizational paralysis, the second in all out mutiny!

What I am suggesting is that vision tends to emerge in a variety of different ways, and through a variety of different people. In some churches, vision is in fact discerned by the lead pastor, but most often vision is discerned through collaboration, often in unexpected ways at unexpected times. But in all cases, regardless of how vision is discerned, three things must happen before advancing a vision beyond ideation:

First, there must be *sufficient* leadership agreement on the vision. The idea is not across-the-board agreement, but ample agreement within the leadership team to legitimately move the vision forward. Pastors are wise to recall the counsel they received when initially exploring the possibility of pastoral ministry, to be sure that others who knew them were affirming of the call they believed had been given to them. Relying on others to affirm (or not) what we believe to be true is uncomfortable and humbling, yet doing so invites the Holy Spirit to speak in and through His people. We may not always like what we hear – King David certainly didn't when the prophet Nathan confronted him about his sin - but it's a vital, faithful step. Inviting other leaders to assess, or to collaboratively develop, a proposed vision will ultimately produce a deep pool of vested leaders who will work diligently to move the vision forward – assuming that there is sufficient leadership agreement on the vision. And while there is no definitive standard for what constitutes "sufficient" leadership agreement, a reasonable guideline is for *at least* 75% of leaders to agree on a proposed vision before advancing it beyond ideation.

Secondly, there must be express agreement from all leaders to promote the vision as a unified, fully committed team. Though some leaders will not fully grasp or have innate passion for the vision, there must be all-in leadership commitment to actively cast and promote the vision. Several years ago, while serving as chairperson of the Board of Deacons at my former church, the lead pastor of the church began to cast a vision for a new worship service. The vision was borne of a deep desire to more effectively reach younger families for Christ. While I shared the pastor's desire to reach these younger families, I disagreed with the new service plant for a variety of reasons - all of which later proved to be unfounded. The experience was humbling and instructive, and I am grateful that the new service did in fact help bring many younger families to Christ. But even as I was wrong in my assessment of the vision, I did manage to get one thing right: after the leadership team voted in favor of the proposal, I immediately pledged my full support, offering to help in any way possible to enable the vision to come to fruition. Leaders must set aside their own preferences in order to stand together in support of vision.

Thirdly, and perhaps most importantly, while the lead pastor does not have to personally discern the vision, he or she must be deeply passionate and wholeheartedly committed to it. The uncomfortable truth is that vision rises or falls with the senior leader, which necessitates that the lead pastor cast and preach the vision frequently, creatively, and passionately. Do this, and the vision will become contagious; don't, and the vision will evaporate.

Vision comes in two forms: specific and directional

A specific vision is one in which there exists a clearly defined end point, where the desired destination is known and can be arrived at. In contrast, a directional vision is one in which there is clarity on a direction to take, but not on a specific destination. When vision is directional, the belief is that during the journey, a specific vision will eventually emerge.

Both types of vision have their place, and both are equally viable, and equally biblical. For example, Moses received a specific vision, which he spoke in Deuteronomy 8:7-10:

> "For the Lord your God is bringing you into a good land — a land with brooks, streams, and deep springs gushing out into the valleys and hills; a land with wheat and barley, vines and fig trees, pomegranates, olive oil and honey; a land where bread will not be scarce and you will lack nothing; a land where the rocks are iron and you can dig copper out of the hills. When you have eaten and are satisfied, praise the Lord your God for the good land he has given you."

This is a vision with a clear, unmistakable end point. The Israelites would know with certainty when they would have arrived at Canaan. Sadly, their sin caused them to wander for forty years rather than make the journey in the eleven or so days it should have taken!

In contrast, the vision given by God to Abram (Abraham) in Genesis 12:1-3 was largely directional:

"The Lord had said to Abram, 'Go from your country, your people and your father's household to the land I will show you. I will make you into a great nation, and I will bless you; I will make your name great, and you will be a blessing. I will bless those who bless you, and whoever curses you I will curse; and all peoples on earth will be blessed through you.'"

And so began the journey of Abram, who with wife Sarai and nephew Lot, set out for Canaan. Never in a million years could Abram have imagined all that God had in store for him. All he knew at the onset is that God called him to a journey, one that would bless him and all peoples. Abram had no inkling that at the ripe old age of 99, and with Sarai at age 90, God would gift him with a son (Isaac). Or that many years later, to test his faith, God would command him to sacrifice his only son, who would be spared at the last moment. Or that the directional vision God gave him in Genesis 12:1-3 would be followed by a more specific vision in Genesis 15:5, in which God tells Abram, "Look up at the sky and count the stars — if indeed you can count them. So shall your offspring be."

Abram believed the Lord, and God credited it to him as righteousness. Indeed, following a directional vision tends to be much more difficult than following a specific vision. We know we're called to step into a journey, but we are not sure where the journey is meant to take us. Trust – in God and in those who join us on the journey – is the order of the day.

Turning from fact to fiction, let us briefly consider the West family. Was their vision specific or directional? The argument for their vision being specific is that they identified Disney World as their ultimate landing spot for a family vacation, and agreed to work toward the vision in the few years after their trip out west. On the other hand, an argument can be made that their vision is directional, given that 1) their western vacation was envisioned as a western *adventure*, where plans would form and solidify as they went along, and 2) while Disney represents what they *assume* to be their dream vacation, it is entirely possible that their experience out west may lead to a new vision.

There is no value in getting hung up on whether the West family established a directional or specific vision, but there is in recognizing that a specific vision always requires a directional *journey* (see Moses, who was forced to endure the direction*less* wandering of the Israelites) … and that a directional vision always leads to specific stops along the way where clarity emerges (see Abraham, who spent the last one-hundred years of his life watching the vision God gave him gradually unfold).

To make practical application, let's imagine a scenario in which two churches are located down the street from one another.

First Church has been in existence for nearly a century, and has a rich history of making disciples in their community and beyond. But in recent years the church has struggled to bring in new people, resulting in a steady decline in both attendance and giving. The leadership at First recently discerned a directional vision to connect the church much more deeply with their community. They are unsure of all that the vision will require, but are ready and willing to begin the journey. They start by establishing a mentoring program with the elementary school down the road, along with a food pantry and midweek dinner program to serve those in need. First Church is journeying in a direction, but where it leads to is anyone's guess. Their challenge is, like Abraham, to believe and follow the path that God has called them to journey on.

New Church is, well, a new church. The church began six years ago by a small group of people who had a shared desire to reach young families in the community. Within its first two years, New Church grew from fifty people in worship to over two-hundred. Four years later, having grown to over five-hundred people in three Sunday worship services, New Church has outgrown its worship center. Hence, the leadership at New Church has discerned and cast a vision for a new worship center that will hold up to 700 people – ideal for where the church finds itself. But amidst the excitement that most in the church feel, some congregants have expressed concern over the church losing its identity, its distinctiveness. The challenge for New Church is to be sure that their journey toward a specific vision is directionally aligned with who they are and what they stand for. Otherwise, they *will* lose their identity, which would be devastating. Matthew 5:13 comes to mind, in which Jesus tells His disciples, "You are the salt of the earth. But if the salt loses its saltiness, how can it be made salty again? It is no longer good for anything, except to be thrown out and trampled underfoot."

Two churches with two very different visions. Is one better than the other? No! Both churches are seeking to be faithful to how they believe God is leading them going forward.

CRAFTING A VISION STATEMENT

You've prayed, you've dreamed, you've discerned, and you've gained ample support from your leadership team. Now it's time to finalize a vision statement.

The worst thing I could do at this point is to instruct you on how to craft a vision statement. Sure, I could probably provide a template that would work to yield an *effective* vision statement, but there is nothing I can give to enable you to craft a vision statement that truly reflects what you have discerned, and that captures the passion you have for the vision.

What I can give you is a basic filter that your vision statement must pass through before you go forward with it. If your vision statement meets the criteria below, you're good to go; if not, I encourage you to go back to the drawing board!

The vision must ...

> *Clearly support the mission.*
> This is a no-brainer, right? Well ... not so fast! Unfortunately, some churches cast a vision that doesn't support the mission, but competes with it for focus and resources. A well-discerned, well-crafted vision will always align with and help bring forth the mission.

> *Honor the existing culture of the church.*
> You've heard the saying, "Don't throw out the baby with the bath water," right? Well, don't! Long standing church members need to feel good (or at least settled) about the past and present in order to get excited about the future.

Don't dwell on how bad things were, or are, in the hope of spurring people to hope for change. It won't work. Rather, honor the past and present while pointing to the future.

Inspire.
If your vision statement doesn't make your heart race a bit faster, it probably needs some work. Enough said.

Be brief and to the point.
Your vision statement should be just that – a statement. Ideally, a vision statement should be easy to memorize. Long, rambling dissertations are anything but.

Be preached.
Is your vision "preachable"? It had better be, because it will need to be preached – time and time and time again. A lead pastor I once worked for used the expression "creative redundancy" to describe the need to send the same message over and over but in a variety of different, creative ways. An inspiring vision statement will lend itself to being creatively and redundantly preached.

QUESTIONS FOR DISCUSSION & REFLECTION

- Do you believe that vision is frequently borne of discontent?

- What sacrifices have you, or your church, made in order to help vision come to fruition?

- Do you agree that vision can be either specific or directional? What sort of vision does your church hold?

9

VALUES

The mission of a church is the call, given by Christ, to go and make disciples. The vision of a church represents what its leaders believe God would have them do in the near future to fulfill the mission. The core values of a church define what it stands for, and what it will endeavor to safeguard through all circumstances, and at all times.

The importance of clearly understood, clearly stated values cannot be overstated. Values are instrumental for helping a church navigate through key decisions, and to preserve what it deems to be most important.

To illustrate, suppose a church has a stated mission grounded in bringing people to Christ and helping people grow to become more like Christ, and a directional vision centered on helping people (especially young adults) in their church and community find wholeness in Christ – spiritually, emotionally, physically, and relationally. Church leaders have discerned six ways to help realize their vision: organized acts of service in neighborhoods and homes; providing monthly childcare at the church to allow neighborhood couples to have a date night; hosting a variety of life-skills workshops; hosting an Alpha program to help seekers safely explore the Christian faith; partnering with community resources to create a low cost counseling voucher program; and partnering with a local fitness center to provide low cost exercise opportunities.

Additionally, the leadership is contemplating a change to its worship style, moving from traditional (organ, hymns) to contemporary (guitar, praise team). The first six ideas were well supported by both leaders and members, but the worship change idea has been met with considerable resistance. There are some – many in fact – who favor the change, but there are others who have been outspoken in their opposition. After two months, the leaders remain divided on whether or not to alter their worship style, prompting the lead pastor to call a special leadership meeting to resolve the stalemate one way or the other. Wisely, Pastor Jones secures agreement from leaders that they will vote to make a firm decision at the meeting.

A few weeks later the meeting takes place. They begin with an extended time of prayer, after which Pastor Jones shares a devotion based on James 1:19. Pastor Jones then restates the church's mission and vision, asking leaders to once again affirm both, which they do with gusto and unanimity. From there the pastor allows thirty minutes for leaders who wish to state their position, and briefly express why they feel as they do. Those who prefer to keep the current worship style express concern over losing some members (which would likely have an adverse effect on giving), breaking with their long-standing tradition and heritage, and losing the excellence in worship that they enjoy today. Those in support of the change cite the challenges the church has faced in bringing in new families, the need to appeal to people based on their preferences rather than the church's, and the need to simply change in general, given the reality of a graying church.

While passing out two pieces of paper to each leader, Pastor Jones explains what will happen next. "Clearly there are strong cases for both keeping worship as is, and changing to contemporary. So we can agree that this is not a matter of right or wrong – both styles are perfectly acceptable, and both bring glory to God. But we have to discern which style is right for us as we go forward. So, we're going to take a few minutes to pray, and afterwards, with as much objectivity as you can bring, I want you to answer two questions. But your answers will come in the form of a numerical rating that you'll give to each of the worship options, and for each of the questions."

Pastor Jones goes on to explain that the scale they'll be using is a simple 5-point scale, with 1 being very unlikely, 2 unlikely, 3 somewhat likely, 4 likely, and 5 highly likely. "Using the 5-point scale for each worship option, the first question is, 'how likely will this style be in helping to bring about mission attainment?'" After a few minutes, he continues. "The second question, again using the 5-point scale for each of the worship styles, is, 'how likely will this style be in helping to bring about vision attainment?'"

A few minutes later the leaders take a short break while Pastor Jones and a few other leaders tally the responses. The group reconvenes, and Pastor Jones speaks. "I need to tell you that as your pastor, I am much less concerned about the style of worship we use than about fulfilling the Great Commission and stepping into the vision we believe God has set before us. I am especially concerned about safeguarding our core values – our core *beliefs* – that make us who we are. I'm telling you this because out of our last exercise, one of the options scored higher than the other. But before we take a final vote, I want us to consider the option in light of our values. I want us to be absolutely sure that this particular approach to worship is not only in line with our values, but that it serves to bring out the very best in what we value."

At this point, I feel the need to temporarily pause our illustration to let you know that I have no intention of telling you which of the two worship options the leaders selected. It's simply not important! Personally, I have experienced the joy of worshipping in Christ-centered, Gospel-proclaiming churches of all types – traditional, contemporary, liturgical, free flowing, formal, informal, structured, unstructured, reserved, charismatic. Worship style is but one of a litany of variables that all churches must address at different points. Worship style is important, but it's also subjective - what works well at one church is ineffective at another.

Okay, back to our illustration. Pastor Jones has guided the leadership team to the brink of making a key decision. But he has wisely asked the leaders to consider running the preferred option through the grid of their core values. He begins: "I'm going to make this part simple. I'm passing out a sheet of paper with our seven core values. I'll read each of them, then give you a moment to write either 'yes', 'no', or 'not sure' next to each. A 'yes' means that you believe this option aligns well and upholds our value; 'no' indicates that you don't believe that the option aligns with and upholds our value; and 'not sure' means just that – not sure."

Recognizing the risk of veering into nebulousness, I'll stop here with our illustration. Hopefully it has proved sufficient to make the simple point that core values serve to guide (or at least filter) key decisions, while safeguarding what is most sacred to a given church. Values matter!

STATED VALUES, ACTUAL VALUES

Have you had the experience of working for an organization that published a list of core values, but in reality fell woefully short of what was listed?

Most of us have, and not just once or twice but on numerous occasions, and in numerous environments. But if we're honest with ourselves, we'll admit that as individuals our tendency is to do the same thing. What's true for companies, and for churches, is also true for people – that far too often what actually *is* lies in stark contrast to what ideally *should be.*

Yet even as we recognize and acknowledge the disconnect between what is and what should be, it is important, especially for organizations, to identify the ideals they aspire to live by, and to list those ideals as *core values.*

Publicly stating our ideals - our core values - provides us with a standard to strive for, and to hold ourselves accountable against. A question that lies ever before us is, "Does what we do align with what we claim to believe?" Getting to "yes" on this question is difficult; staying at "yes" is nearly impossible. But to honestly, earnestly *strive* for alignment between what we do and what we believe is of much greater significance than the actual results. God doesn't keep score on us; God searches our hearts. And, thankfully, God does not judge us according to our own righteousness, but on whether or not we receive the righteousness offered to us in Christ.

Invariably, we fall short time and time again. But if we truly, earnestly desire to live in accordance with what we value, we avoid the snare of hypocrisy. On that note, the problem with the Pharisees wasn't so much that they were wrong, but that they didn't have an honest desire to do what was right. Their *stated* values were in line with the Word of God, but their hearts were not, leaving a vast chasm between stated and actual values. To illustrate ...

THE PHARISEES ...	
Stated Value	Actual Value
Purity	Tradition and Selectivity
(Phil. 3:4-6; Mt. 15:2; Acts 26:5)	(Mt. 15:1-9; Mt. 23:4; Jn. 7:21-24)
Righteousness	Judgmentalism
(Mt. 9:10-11; Lk. 15:2; Mt. 5:20)	(Lk. 18:9-14; Jn. 8:1-6)
Godliness	Selfishness
(Mt. 23:2; Acts 23:6-10; Mt. 15:8)	(Mt. 23:5-7; Jn. 12:42-43; Mt. 27:18)
Sacrifice	Greed
(Mt. 23:23a, 25a)	(Mt. 23:23b-24, 25b-26; Lk. 16:14)

Note that each of the stated values above are good, even holy, values. But because their hearts were not set on God but on themselves, the Pharisees actual values stood in stark contrast to their stated values (and in fairness, even if their hearts had been set on God, the Pharisees would still have fallen short of their stated values – we all do and desperately need the grace of God). Jesus saved His harshest criticism for the Pharisees, because they lacked earnestness.

CORE BELIEFS, CORE VALUES

It only makes sense that what we most ardently believe, we should most ardently value. This is straightforward, but the reality for many churches is that there exists a sizable gap between core beliefs and core values. The foremost cause, as I see it, is a failure to clearly differentiate core beliefs from secondary beliefs, and for that matter core values from secondary values.

Core beliefs are what we believe to be *absolutely* true, and worth holding on to at all costs. Hence, core values must be rooted in and established from core beliefs (the two are so intertwined that most churches publish either core beliefs or core values as a single list, rather than two separate lists, a practice that I find to be appropriate and acceptable).

In contrast, secondary beliefs are what we *believe* to be true, but are at least somewhat open to changing. Secondary values emerge from secondary beliefs, with both held loosely, open to change over the course of time. And as is the case with core beliefs and core values, secondary beliefs and secondary values are intertwined. However, unlike core beliefs and values, I do not recommend that secondary beliefs and values merit a specific listing.

Clearly understanding what we hold as core – as *foundational, fixed* – and setting those beliefs apart from what we hold as secondary – as *changeable* - is of vital importance. A failure to distinguish core beliefs and values from secondary beliefs and values conveys that everything is either up for grabs or frozen. Hence, core beliefs and values that should be fixed are subject to change, while secondary beliefs and values that should be subject to change remain fixed.

Delineation between core and secondary is vital for avoiding directionless ambiguity. A core value should express the big idea – what we believe and aspire to – but not the secondary details of *how* we go about fulfilling the core value. Easy enough, but I have seen churches list secondary values as core values (and vice-versa), which makes sorting out the foundational from the changeable a difficult, subjective task.

VALUES SHOULD REPRESENT WHAT WE ARE FOR (NOT WHAT WE ARE AGAINST)

A mistake that some churches make, and that hinders the witness of the church, is to focus more on what we stand against, rather than what we stand for.

Like it or not, there exists a strong anti-church (and anti-Christian) bias in today's culture. Much of the bias comes with the territory – after all, Jesus never said it would be easy to be His disciple (see John 15:18-25). But in truth, individuals and whole churches bring much of the anti-Christian, anti-church bias on themselves by being quick to demonstrate what they stand against, and slow to demonstrate what – and who – they stand for.

Our example is Christ, who consistently spoke and acted in accordance with what He stood for, rather than against. Jesus made His intentions clear from the start, when He announced His ministry by quoting from Isaiah:

> "The Spirit of the Lord is on me, because he has anointed me to proclaim good news to the poor. He has sent me to proclaim freedom for the prisoners and recovery of sight for the blind, to set the oppressed free, to proclaim the year of the Lord's favor." (Luke 4:18-19)

Shortly thereafter, Matthew 5:3-10 records that Jesus, preaching from an unnamed mountainside, makes crystal clear what (and who) He stands for:

> "Blessed are the poor in spirit,
>> for theirs is the kingdom of heaven.
> Blessed are those who mourn,
>> for they will be comforted.
> Blessed are the meek,
>> for they will inherit the earth.
> Blessed are those who hunger and thirst for righteousness,
>> for they will be filled.
> Blessed are the merciful,
>> for they will be shown mercy.
> Blessed are the pure in heart,
>> for they will see God.
> Blessed are the peacemakers,
>> for they will be called children of God.
> Blessed are those who are persecuted because of righteousness,
>> for theirs is the kingdom of heaven."

In fairness, throughout the course of His ministry, Jesus did in fact make clear that He stood against religious hypocrisy. But even as Jesus railed against the hypocrisy of the religious leaders of the day, His love for them was never in question. Incredibly, as Jesus hung on a cross near death, He expressed His love for those who crucified Him, saying "Father, forgive them, for they do not know what they are doing" (Luke 23:34). Jesus came to bring life, not condemnation.

But what about us? Do we, like Jesus, emphasize what we are for, rather than against? Or are we like the Pharisees, fixated on what we stand against?

The tragedy in being against so much is that others fail to see a clear picture of the One we claim to be for. People don't see Christ in us because our words and actions don't reflect Christ. And make no mistake, the unchurched and de-churched people we interact with associate us – for better or worse - with Christ and His church. What we think, say, and do matters greatly. When we convey what (and who) we are for, people see Christ in us. When we convey what (and who) we are against, people see religiosity at its worst.

ATTRACTIVE, NOT ATTRACTIONAL

At the risk of offending some, I am closing this chapter with an editorial. It seems to me that the word "attractional" has received a whole lot of bad press in church circles over the past decade or so. In fact, if you google the word, you'll notice two things straight away: first, that the only context *attractional* seems to be used in is in church/ministry, and second, that being "attractional" is almost always set against being "missional," as if every church must choose between one or the other. So what gives?

Let's start by stating the obvious: a church had better be missional, otherwise the church isn't truly functioning as a church, and arguably isn't fit to be called a church. But the question remains: Can an attractional church be a missional church?

My answer is no. An "attractional" church is one that elevates attractiveness as its *primary* focus, rather than heeding the call of Christ. An attractional church is one that might be very wide (lots of people, big programs, cutting edge worship, etc.), yet spiritually shallow, as evidenced by a lack of conversions, a weak or non-existent discipleship culture, and front and back doors that are constantly revolving.

But, let's not stop there. Because in truth a church can – and *must* – be attractive in order to be optimally missional. The difference is in understanding that attraction is not the big idea, but rather a means to a greater end. Our primary focus cannot – *ever* – be on making our church attractive, but must always be on making disciples. Being an attractive church is a positive characteristic, assuming of course that "attraction" serves as a gateway to bring people in, *and* bring them to Christ, *and* grow them in Christ, *and* encourage and teach them to be ambassadors for Christ. When this dynamic is present, there develops a profound, powerful awareness in people that what is most attractive - by far - is what God has done, is doing, and will do still. *That* kind of attraction isn't fleeting, but lasting.

One last point. If a church is attractional, the language most often heard is typically along the lines of, "come and look at." But if a church is attractive, the language you'll hear is along the lines of, "come and see." Are you catching the difference? To invite someone to "come and look at" is in essence inviting them to check out what we have done - come and look at our building, our programs, our worship facility, and so on. But inviting someone to "come and see" shifts the focus to God - come and see what God is doing! Come and see how God is working at His church! Come and see how God is changing lives! Come and see ... just come and see. God will show up, because He always shows up. And *that* is attractive.

QUESTIONS FOR DISCUSSION & REFLECTION

- Describe the difference between core values and secondary values.

- Why is it important for core values to take precedence over secondary values?

- Do the values at your church help or hinder the mission?

10

LONG-RANGE PLANS

When a vision is complex and/or far-reaching, long-range plans help bring cohesion, ongoing focus, and steady progress relative to the vision.

To illustrate, several years ago, while I was serving at Beechwood Church in Holland, Michigan, the leadership of the church came under conviction that the Lord was calling us to step out in faith more deeply than ever before. Under the leadership of our lead pastor Jim Lankheet, and following a long season of prayer and dialogue, a vision began to crystalize.

What started as a directional vision - to do everything we could to help as many people as possible experience a changed life in Christ – soon became a specific, *God-sized* vision consisting of four intertwined large-scale initiatives: church planting on a regular, cyclical basis; a significantly enhanced outdoor worship venue; major property enhancements (including a lodge) to allow for increased and more effective outdoor ministry; and implementation of a wholeness ministry designed to help people live full, healthy, Christ-centered lives.

The church identified three other ongoing priorities – mission support, ministry enhancements, and debt reduction – and combined the four new initiatives with the three ongoing priorities to introduce a church-wide vision & capital campaign called "Opportunities."

But whereas the three ongoing priorities were largely a continuation of what was already taking place, the four new initiatives required a significant level of planning. These initiatives were treated as long-range plans, allowing for a common, agreed upon understanding of key milestones, deliverables, and implementation stages for each. By the grace of God, when the capital campaign concluded three years later, each of the seven "opportunities" were realized, and many lives have in fact been changed through these vital ministries.[20]

As previously mentioned, I consider long-range plans to be optional during the planning process. In many cases, especially when a vision has been in place for quite some time and the annual planning process is consistently effective, long-range plans are unnecessary; in other cases, particularly when a vision is complex and stretching, long-range plans can be a vital way to bridge the gap between vision and annual plans.

PART FOUR

ANNUAL PLANNING

"All hard work brings a profit, but mere talk leads only to poverty."
(Proverbs 14:23)

L et's pause for a moment to reflect on where we are, and where we go from here. You began with a time of preparation, praying for the Holy Spirit to guide and direct your leaders and church in this season, and acknowledging afresh the supremacy of Christ and centrality of the Gospel. You established a planning timeline to keep you focused and on track. You have taken a long look into the mirror of your church, objectively assessing its effectiveness both in bringing people to Christ, and helping people grow to become more like Christ. Your staff and lay leaders are on board and committed to seeking and following the leading of the Holy Spirit. You've established (or recommitted to) a mission rooted in the Great Commission, and have clarity (or are gaining clarity) on a vision, be it specific or directional. Your core values are embraced by key leaders, and there is a shared desire to function in accordance with what you value. Finally, you have begun to consider what it might entail to move from "here" to "there" as a church.

Give yourself a moment to catch your breath! As you do, allow me to congratulate you on what you have accomplished to this point. The investment you have made in preparation, assessment, and long-range planning will serve you well as you segue into annual planning.

But along with congratulations, I must also pass along a word of caution: the surest way to squander an investment is to lose your zeal to optimize it. Settling for "good enough" is simply not an option for leaders in Christ's church. Your challenge is to pour as much energy and focus into annual planning as you did in preparation, assessment, and long-range planning.

Simply put, effective leadership is predicated on diligent leadership. In Romans 12, the Apostle Paul makes this very point in an interesting and creative way. Beginning in verse 6, Paul lists the various gifts that members of the body bring to the whole: "If your gift is prophesying, then prophesy ... if it is serving, then serve ... if it is teaching, then teach ... if it is to encourage, then give encouragement ... if it is giving, then give generously..."

If you're keeping score, your scorecard looks something like this: Prophets prophesy, servants serve, teachers teach, encouragers encourage, givers give. But then, in verse 8, Paul throws a curveball: "If it is to lead, do it diligently."

Prophets prophesy, servants serve, teachers teach, encouragers encourage, givers give, and leaders lead ... *diligently*. Effective leaders do not accept "good enough" as being good enough, and are never content with remaining in place. Rather, effective leaders prayerfully and actively press on, trusting the Lord and doing their best to be in lockstep with God every step of the way.

And so it is, with the foundational elements of mission, vision, values, and (optionally) long-range plans in place, we turn our focus to discerning annual objectives and strategies. Let us begin by refreshing our understanding of what each element represents:

Objectives answer the question of what God is leading us to do in the coming year to be faithful to the mission, step toward the vision, and uphold our values. Objectives are established (or carried over) annually and communicated dynamically.

Strategies answer the question of what we will do in the coming year to achieve the objectives. Typically, strategies are set annually in conjunction with establishing objectives. Strategies can be altered, stopped, or added during the year as the Holy Spirit leads.

THERE'S AN APP (ANNUAL PLANNING PROCESS) FOR THAT

While there are a variety of approaches that can be used for annual planning, finding an approach that rightly balances spirituality with practicality has proven to be an exercise in frustration for many pastors and leaders, including yours truly. However, borne of many lessons learned through many planning seasons, I have developed a straightforward, effective annual planning process that I call "5-for-5."

5-for-5 is built around five steps that in combination guide your leadership team to discern no more than five objectives, each supported by no more than five strategies. The steps build on one another, helping to produce annual plans that are inspired by the Holy Spirit and surrendered to God.

In the pages that follow we will examine the steps in detail, but for now here is a basic summary: [21]

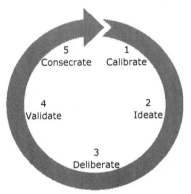

Step 1: Calibrate. Before putting pen to paper, we must be intentional to fix our focus on God rather than ourselves.

Step 2: Ideate. This is when creative juices run freely, and ideas emerge in rapid fashion.

Step 3: Deliberate. Here we categorize, scrutinize, and prioritize, selectively converting ideas into plans.

Step 4: Validate. Before we lock in objectives and strategies, we pause to ensure that our work aligns with and supports our mission, vision, and values.

Step 5: Consecrate. Finally, we surrender our plans to God, praying and expecting that God will bless and prosper our work, according to His good will and purpose.

There is latitude in how you choose to approach the 5-for-5 steps. Some leadership teams meet for three hours on two separate occasions, covering steps 1 and 2 during the first session, and steps 3, 4 and 5 during the second. Other teams meet weekly for 90 minutes over a four-week period, covering steps 1 and 2 during the first two sessions, step 3 in the third session, and steps 4 and 5 in the fourth session. Still others cover all of the steps during a weekend retreat.

Whatever approach you take, be careful not to rush through the process. Each step is vital! If you feel rushed, add an extra meeting to slow the process down and get it right. After all, a few more hours of work is a small price to pay for a well discerned annual plan.

While acknowledging that 5-for-5 lends itself to a variety of approaches, experience reveals that the best results tend to come through engaging all of the steps during a single weekend retreat. Retreats have a way of moving us closer to God and each other, bringing both camaraderie and results. Calibration comes through extended, unhurried times of prayer, worship and study, which position the team for success in ideation, deliberation, and validation. And it's hard to imagine a better way of consecrating our work to God than by closing a retreat with a time of sacred worship and Holy Communion.

Whatever you do, don't delay in selecting an approach, and scheduling and communicating the dates to leaders. Better yet, at the onset of Phase 1 (Preparation) of the overall planning process, schedule a weekend retreat to take place in Phase 4 (Annual Planning). This way you and your leaders will be positioned for a successful annual planning process.

11

CALIBRATION

calibrate: to adjust precisely to a particular function

It is imperative that before we start down the path of ideation, we calibrate our heart and mind to the things of God. Calibration – and recalibration, and recalibration, and recalibration - is essential because of our human tendency to drift from God. This is especially true during strategic planning, when the fatigue of a long and taxing journey can move us to focus more on what we want than on what God desires to do in and through us.

In general, we calibrate our hearts and minds by following the same core spiritual disciplines that have been used for centuries – prayer, scripture meditation, worship, and serving. But calibration as it relates to strategic planning necessitates, in my estimation, a more intentional approach of looking up, looking back, and looking around, before looking ahead. Looking up connects us to God, looking back renews our trust in God, and looking around reveals how God is currently at work, all of which bring spiritual acuity as we look ahead.

LOOK UP

First things first: Before putting pen to paper - or fingers to keyboard, or marker to whiteboard – take time to pray. I realize that I am stating the obvious, but experience has taught me that more often than we care to admit, pastors and leaders are quicker to roll up their sleeves and go to work than to get on their knees and pray.

But faith-based plans require faith-based leaders who stay connected to God through prayer, worship, and scripture. To calibrate your heart and mind to the things of God, here are some specific things that you and your leadership team can pray for and meditate on:

Bringing glory to God

"So whether you eat or drink or whatever you do, do it all for the glory of God." (1 Corinthians 10:31)

Trust

"Trust in the Lord with all your heart and lean not on your own understanding." (Proverbs 29:25)

Wisdom

"If you need wisdom, ask our generous God, and he will give it to you." (James 1:5)

The leading of the Holy Spirit

"For those who are led by the Spirit of God are the children of God." (Romans 8:14)

Perseverance

> "Let us not become weary in doing good, for at the proper time we will reap a harvest if we do not give up." (Gal. 6:9)

Faith

> "Now faith is confidence in what we hope for and assurance about what we do not see." (Hebrews 11:1)

"Looking up" can be accomplished in a variety of ways. You might consider holding an extended prayer vigil, where individual leaders sign up to pray during a specific time interval. Or a special worship service for church leaders, where prayer and praise foster a deeper connection with God. Or a day of fasting and scripture meditation. Or simply leaving it up to each person to determine their own approach. How you do it is up to you, but be sure to "look up" before proceeding.

> "You will seek me and find me when you seek me with all your heart." (Jeremiah 29:13)

LOOK BACK

Confidence and assurance for what lies ahead is rooted in understanding and appreciating what has already taken place. The whole of scripture reveals the breathtaking dimensions of God's unfolding plan of redemption and restoration, which is assured in Christ.

Scripture connects what was with what is, and what is yet to come. Knowing what has already taken place, and what is promised, instills in us a deeper understanding that God is indeed sovereign, that Christ is indeed building His Church, and that the Holy Spirit is indeed bringing about transformation.

Romans 15:4 conveys this dynamic beautifully:

> "Everything that was written in the past was written to teach us, so that through endurance and the encouragement of the Scriptures we might have hope."

The unfolding biblical narrative is ample in itself to strengthen us for what lies ahead. But let's not stop there; let's make it personal. Whether your church has been in existence for two years or two-hundred years, God has been at work throughout its history. Before forming ideas and plans, pause to reflect on and be strengthened by recalling how God has worked in your church. Think on days past when God's providence was unmistakable and God's movement undeniable.

In fact, why not gather your leaders for a time of prayer, reflection, and thanksgiving in a specific place in your church or community where God was clearly at work in the past? It could be the sanctuary that God provided at a point in time. It could be the building the church used to worship at prior to its present location. It could be a meeting room where an important leadership decision was made many years ago. What place in your church or community can you gather your leaders to help remind them of God's faithfulness?

The precedent for this approach was set by Christ Himself. Just prior to His death, Jesus instructed the Disciples to meet Him on a specific mountain in Galilee following His resurrection (Mt. 26:32, Mt. 28:16). Meeting on a mountain would have made for a difficult, uncomfortable journey, but Jesus called the disciples there because throughout the Scriptures, time and time again, God reveals who He is on mountains. God gave the Ten Commandments on Mount Sinai; God reigned down fire on Mount Carmel; Jesus was transfigured on a "high mountaintop." In bringing the Disciples to a mountain in Galilee, Jesus takes them back to the origins of their faith. It was in Galilee that Jesus first called most of them, performed His first public miracle, and preached the Sermon on the Mount. Jesus knew the importance of having His disciples look back before receiving the commission He would give them while on the mountain:

> "Go and make disciples of all nations, baptizing them in the name of the Father and of the Son and of the Holy Spirit, and teaching them to obey everything I have commanded you." (Mt. 28:19-20)

Where is your mountaintop? What place will you gather the leaders in your church to reflect on and be strengthened by who God is, and what God has done?

LOOK AROUND

Calibrating our heart and mind requires us to not only look up and look back, but to look around. How do you see God working right now? What is God doing that you can join in and build upon?

My dual role with the Reformed Church in America Classis of North Grand Rapids, and Region of the Great Lakes, takes me into a great number of churches. One of the things I am most impressed with is the variety of creative, highly effective ministries at our churches. There are community gardens, homeless shelters, neighborhood meals, food pantries, public school mentoring programs, housing assistance initiatives, education and job training workshops, financial management classes, complimentary tax return services, leadership development programs, recovery groups, and much more. In fact, what I have listed here barely scratches the surface! But I'll stop because my intent is not to spotlight ministries, but to point out how effective ministries are birthed.

With rare exceptions, when I ask a pastor or leader to explain what led them to start a given ministry, they allude to two factors: recognition of a legitimate need within the church or community, and recognition that God was already inspiring people to serve while providing an onramp for the church to get involved.

If your desire is to impact your church and community for Christ, then look around before looking ahead. Looking around calibrates us to the intersection between community needs and how God is working to inspire and call His people.

QUESTIONS FOR DISCUSSION & REFLECTION

- Is it possible to discern faith-based plans without *looking up?*

- Think about one of your existing ministries or programs that might be considered "out of the box." When the ministry or program started, how was God at work in the church or community? What led the church to begin the ministry or program? Does recalling what took place at that time provide a lesson for the church today?

12

IDEATION

ideate: to form an idea

On your mark, get set ... pause. Don't worry – my intention is not to stick a pin in your ever burgeoning balloon of creativity, but to help your time spent in ideation be wildly successful. Because while ideation is about letting creative juices flow and ideas fly, like anything else, it must be managed. And so before we ideate, let us first consider how to prepare for ideation.

PREPARING FOR IDEATION

One key to effective preparation is to clearly understand and avoid the two poles that make for *ineffective* preparation.

On one side is *under-preparation*. I don't need to describe in detail how an under-prepared facilitator impacts ideation because I am certain you already know. Just about everyone has experienced the frustration of participating in a group brainstorming session where the facilitator didn't clearly outline what the goal of the session was ... or provide key background information relative to the topic ... or hold the meeting in an environment conducive to creativity. Speaking from experience, facilitators who are under-prepared don't arrive there by accident. Rather, their focus leading up to ideation is on other matters that *seem* more important, leaving little or no capacity to plan for successful ideation. Thinking back to the Time Matrix covered in Part 3, preparation clearly fits in Quadrant II, meriting our attention but only getting it if we elevate preparation from an "as time allows" activity to a "must do" priority.

Over-preparation occupies the other side of the ineffective planning spectrum. An over-prepared facilitator (or participant) has researched the task at hand to the nth degree, thinking through every possible solution, and believing beyond a shadow of doubt that they know what needs to happen. But because they clutch their ideas too tightly, others in the room shut down and check out of the process altogether.

Knowing what we ought not to do, let's now turn our attention to what we *must* do to adequately prepare for ideation.

Identify a facilitator

While the lead pastor typically leads the overall planning process, ideation may be facilitated by any leader who is skilled in facilitation and familiar with the church's mission, vision, values, and long-range plans (if applicable). In the Ideation Process that follows, we'll delve into how to facilitate ideation, but proactively identifying and enlisting a facilitator who demonstrates the following characteristics is a necessary first step:

   ✓ Widely respected and appreciated by other leaders;
   ✓ Comfortable with remaining neutral on key issues;
   ✓ Strong listening and processing skills;
   ✓ Able to clearly convey structure, process and goals;

✓ Gifted at optimizing participation and interaction;

✓ Committed to fostering a safe environment, free of judgement or condemnation;

✓ Skilled at asking questions that encourage creativity and help build on stated ideas;

✓ Easily adaptable, able to move in concert with the conversation.

Meet with key leaders

As soon as a facilitator is identified, he or she should connect with a few key leaders, most notably the lead pastor if the pastor isn't facilitating ideation. These meetings should be brief – no more than thirty minutes – with a goal of simply establishing agreement on essential details such as approach, environment, time allowed, and devotional content. The intent is to ensure alignment with, and gain support from, key leaders.

Select an environment conducive to creativity

The location you select for ideation is important! The room should be bright, spacious, and free of distractions, offering good sound quality and ample wall space to hang flipchart pages. If you are covering annual planning during a weekend retreat, select a facility that offers a private, comfortable lodge or meeting room.

Assemble completed *Faith-Based* tools

Now is the time to gather and get reacquainted with the work you have already completed. Start rounding up whatever tools you have used - the Spiritual Farming worksheet, Deep and Wide exercise, Vision Convergence worksheet, S.W.O.T. analysis, Here-to-There worksheet, external assessment, etc. Keep reading to learn *how* the tools are used, but at this juncture what we are after is to simply gather and review the work that has been completed.

Gather necessary supplies

At a minimum, you'll need a couple of easels to go with at least two fully stocked flipcharts, several packages of sticky notes, and notepads and pens for all participants. I recommend bringing some fun props such as koosh balls, tinker toys, and building blocks to stimulate creativity. If you are planning on showing videos, using Powerpoint, or having a person scribe and display notes during the session, be sure to reserve a data projector. And bring plenty of light snacks and beverages (or better yet, consider serving a meal in advance of ideation).

Communicate in advance ... then do it again ... and once more for good measure

I can't stress enough how important it is to communicate concisely and creatively on multiple occasions leading up to ideation. Communication should be both verbal and written, exuding enthusiasm and building anticipation, yet also providing important details such as date, time, location, etc. Make a point of informing participants that ideation will start promptly and end on time, and that all leaders are required to participate fully and actively. If meals are being served, highlight that in your communication. And send along the *Faith-Based* tools you have completed, encouraging participants to revisit their work while praying for the Holy Spirit to give direction on what might come next.

THE IDEATION PROCESS

I don't consider myself to be a jazz aficionado, but having two sons who have played jazz for several years has given me something of a front row seat to this rather extraordinary style of music. Jazz is both planned and spontaneous, with musicians playing a given tune but reacting in the moment to the playing of one another and to the vibe they feel. It's in this place, where structure mixes with freedom, history with experimentation, and memorization with improvisation, that the sweet sounds of jazz emerge and take shape.

Like good jazz, good ideation happens when order and structure mesh with spontaneity and creativity. The key is enlisting a facilitator who is adept at keeping the process focused yet fluid. With that in mind, the process steps that follow represent a flexible guideline rather than a rigid process. Feel free to follow all of the steps, or to take an ala carte approach – whatever you feel works best to tap into the creative energies of your leadership team.

1. *Create an atmosphere that encourages creativity.*

    The facilitator should plan on arriving at least an hour before everyone else. Chairs should be comfortable, angled toward the front of the room, and spaced to allow participants room to stretch out a bit. Sticky notes and pens should be placed on or in front of chairs. The props you purchased during preparation should be set out and easily accessible. A welcome poster or slide is a nice touch, as is upbeat music playing as participants walk in. Easels with flipcharts should be strategically placed and ready for use. If you are serving a meal, verify that the meal will be ready to serve at the onset of the session. If you opt to serve snacks and beverages, be sure to brew more coffee than you think you'll need, and place food and drinks in an area that is easily accessible without causing disruption. If you are using video and/or audio equipment, make a point of testing and calibrating the equipment in advance.

2. *Welcome participants and give a brief overview.*

In accordance with prior communication, start the session on time. Do whatever it takes to get people in seats - turn the lights off and on a few times, blow a whistle, turn down the music – whatever it takes! After welcoming your leaders, give a *brief* overview of what the team will be doing during ideation. Walking briskly through an agenda works well provided that you don't linger on any of the points.

3. *Prayer, Worship, and Teaching.*

Take around thirty minutes to pray, worship, and learn together. Start by getting people on their feet and singing, then segue into a brief devotional teaching, selecting scripture that invites reflection and points to the importance of planning. Consider allowing ten to fifteen minutes to break into small groups to allow people to go deeper with the lesson.

4. *Explain the process.*

By now your leaders are spiritually attuned and anxious to begin. But first, take a moment to explain the process of ideation, starting with a few basic rules of brainstorming, namely: That there are no bad ideas; that our task is not to critique or defend ideas (that comes later); that building on other ideas is welcomed and encouraged; and that the goal is to produce a lot of ideas (quantity over quality). Let participants know that because focus is paramount and our time limited, as the facilitator you will be redirecting the discussion at various points. Inform participants that delineating between objectives and strategies is not necessary during ideation, as that will happen later in the process. Finally, display or distribute completed *Faith-Based* tools, reminding leaders that the work completed to this point should help spur ideas.

5. *Begin the process.*

Now you're ready! Inform your leaders that their task is to answer a single question, as displayed on a slide, flipchart, or whiteboard. The question is …

Understanding that our mission – the reason we exist as a church - is to [Mission Statement] …

and that our vision – what God is calling us to be and do in the coming years – is to [Vision Statement] …

and that our (optional) long-range plans, which we believe are vital for realizing the vision, are to [Long-Range Plans] …

and that objectives and strategies represent what God is leading us to do in the coming year to be faithful to the mission and step toward the vision …

What do we sense the Holy Spirit calling us to do in the coming year?

As the facilitator guides the process – asking leading questions, encouraging and affirming participation, keeping the focus on the question at hand, even pausing to pray when the well starts to run dry – ideas flow and themes emerge.

6. *End the process.*

It is good practice to give a five-minute warning as you near the end of ideation, followed by an additional five minutes for participants to write down any final ideas on the sticky notes you provided earlier. Before closing in prayer, thank leaders for participating and inform them of next steps, which are:

That a few leaders will be meeting to sort the ideas into common themes (we'll cover how to do this in Deliberation);

That as common themes emerge, the sub-group will make a first attempt at listing draft objectives and strategies;

That at our next meeting we will enter into the Deliberation phase, when we scrutinize the proposed objectives and strategies in detail in order to settle on no more than five objectives, each supported by no more than five strategies.

QUESTIONS FOR DISCUSSION & REFLECTION

- Why is effective preparation so vital for successful ideation?

- What characteristics should an Ideation facilitator possess?

- In what ways can we invite the Holy Spirit into the ideation process?

13

DELIBERATION

**deliberate: to think about or discuss something very
carefully in order to make a decision**

*"As was his custom, Paul went into the synagogue, and on three
Sabbath days he reasoned with them from the scriptures..."*
(Acts 17:2)

It is interesting and significant that the first four (of six) mentions of the word "reasoned" in Scripture take place in the Book of Acts and involve the Apostle Paul reasoning with a variety of people in a variety of synagogues – Thessalonica (17:1-3), Athens (17:16-18), Corinth (18:1-3), and Ephesus (18:18-20). Paul proclaimed the Gospel everywhere he went, but always in the context of the whole of scripture, understanding that to change a heart you must first change a mind.

Deliberation is very much a reasoning-centered step. While our aim is simple - to selectively convert ideas into plans that align with our mission and guide us toward our vision – our task is anything but. Deliberation by its nature invites disagreement, which for a leadership team lacking in maturity can open the door to division. But for a leadership team that is fully committed to advancing the cause of Christ *while* preserving their unity in Christ, deliberation can bring a team together like never before.

Relative to annual planning, the process of Deliberation involves three fundamental aspects, which chronologically are to categorize, scrutinize, and prioritize. We categorize the ideas received during ideation to formulate an initial list of proposed objectives and strategies; we scrutinize the proposed objectives and strategies in order to refine and shape them; and we prioritize our work to settle on no more than five objectives, each supported by no more than five strategies.

CATEGORIZE

The task of categorizing ideas is best undertaken by a small sub-team of two to four leaders. This team should include the lead pastor and ideation facilitator (if different from the pastor), along with at least one person who is gifted administratively. Because this team has the important task of converting ideas into proposed objectives and strategies, those who are on the team must be highly respected and trusted by other leaders. Further, the person who leads the team should be experienced in strategic planning, a holistic thinker with an ability to make order out of chaos, and simplicity out of complexity.

I recommend allowing around two hours to complete the process of categorizing ideas. If you have scheduled multiple meetings for annual planning, plan on categorizing ideas within a few days of ideation. If you are covering annual planning in a single weekend retreat, categorizing ideas usually takes place during an extended break following ideation.

Regarding how to categorize ideas, here is an approach that is simple yet effective:

1. *Pray for the leading of the Holy Spirit, and for courage to follow where the Spirit leads.*

   In excel (or a whiteboard if you prefer), set up five columns, using the following as column headers: Worship, Discipleship, Fellowship, Service, and Evangelism. (NOTE: These are commonly accepted as core purposes of the church. If your church uses other terms that correspond to any of these, feel free to use what you have).

2. *Look for ideas that are ministry or department specific, and move them to a separate list.*

   For most churches, these ministry/departments include some combination of children's ministry, youth ministry, young adult ministry, senior's ministry, women's ministry, men's ministry, and office/administration. NOT included are ministries that fall directly under any of the five purposes. The reason for segregating ideas that are specific to a ministry or department is that our initial focus must be broad rather than narrow. Objectives and strategies must overarch ministry/department plans, which is why the latter are discerned during the Alignment phase, after objectives and strategies are finalized. But rest assured that ministry/department-specific ideas are not being discarded, just set aside for later consideration.

3. *List each of the remaining ideas in the column they most naturally fit.*

> I recognize that some ideas – maybe most ideas – impact multiple purposes, but our aim is to identify the purpose that would likely be most impacted by the idea.

4. *Taking each column separately, look through the ideas to identify themes.*

> For example, if in the Worship column there is an idea to "Enhance our stage lighting to better match the worship experience," another idea to "Improve sound quality by installing some noise controlling panels," and still another idea to "Place a few decorative tables in the back of the worship center to make it more inviting," there is clearly a theme along the lines of "Enhancing the worship environment." It is not uncommon to identify upwards of ten to fifteen themes as you sift through ideas.

5. *Formulate proposed objectives.*

> Here we examine themes individually and in combination to assess their suitability as proposed objectives. As a reminder, objectives represent at a high level (broad, overarching) what we sense God leading us to do in the coming year to be faithful to the mission and step toward the vision. While the end goal is to discern no more than five objectives, at this point we are free to generate up to twice that amount. But discernment remains essential. For example, I would

contend that the "Enhancing the worship environment" theme identified in our prior example is too narrow in itself to be used as an objective. However, if an additional theme centered on altering our worship style were to emerge, a strong argument could be made to propose an objective to, "Enhance the overall worship experience." Think broadly rather than narrowly when formulating proposed objectives.

6. *Identify strategies.*

Having established a list of proposed objectives, we now turn our focus to identifying strategies. You'll recall that strategies represent what we believe must happen in order to achieve our objectives. Even as strategies are focused solely on helping to achieve a given objective, we must be cautious to not create strategies that are too narrow. After all, what we want are strategies, not tactics. To illustrate, think back to our prior example of proposing an objective to "Enhance the overall worship experience." In essence, the objective encompassed two intertwined themes: to "Enhance the worship environment," and to "Alter the worship style." And while we didn't identify the specific ideas that led to the latter theme, we did identify the ideas that led to the former theme. Those ideas were: "Enhance our stage lighting to better match the worship experience," "Improve sound quality by installing some noise controlling panels," and "Place a few decorative tables in the back of the worship center to make it more inviting."

Now the question: What strategies might we propose to help realize our objective of enhancing the overall worship experience? Our first inclination might be to list our three ideas relative to worship environment, along with other ideas relative to worship style. But while these are fine ideas, they may be too narrow to list as strategies. For example, enhancing our stage lighting is helpful, but would we be better served to consider the appearance of the stage as a whole? And adding noise controlling panels will likely improve sound quality, but are there other variables we should consider as well? And adding a few tables might make our worship center more inviting, but have we given ample thought to the appearance of the worship center as a whole?

A case can be made that the two themes we identified – to "Enhance the worship environment," and to "Alter the worship style" – are much better strategies than the individual ideas themselves. Theme-based strategies honor and take into account the ideas discerned, but are open-ended such that they can be considered more holistically.

SCRUTINIZE

With the sub-team having completed its work of categorizing ideas into proposed objectives and strategies, it's time for the whole leadership team to gather once again. This time, their task is to discuss, debate, and more deeply discern the proposed objectives and strategies that have been set before them.

The starting point is for the sub-team to explain the process they took in categorizing ideas into objectives and strategies. There should be clarity as to why ideas were categorized as they were, and how the sub-team went about doing so.

Before jumping into discussion, be sure to pray once again for the leading of the Holy Spirit to be made clear, and that your conversation would bless the Lord. It is also a good idea to briefly touch on a few biblical tenets of healthy conversation, such as:

Be nice!
"Finally, all of you be harmonious, sympathetic, affectionate, compassionate, and humble." (1 Peter 3:8)

Be open to the counsel of others
"Where there is no guidance, a people falls, but in an abundance of counselors there is safety." (Proverbs 11:14)

Listen for the Holy Spirit
"And your ears shall hear a word behind you, saying, 'This is the way, walk in it,' when you turn to the right or when you turn to the left." (Isaiah 30:21)

Remember what wisdom is, and where it comes from
"But the wisdom from above is first pure, then peaceable, gentle, open to reason, full of mercy and good fruits, impartial and sincere." (James 3:17)

Listen well, and keep your emotions in check

"My dear brothers and sisters, take note of this: Everyone should be quick to listen, slow to speak and slow to become angry." (James 1:19)

Recognize and embrace the diversity of giftedness and thought in your leadership team

"To each one the manifestation of the Spirit is given for the common good. To one there is given through the Spirit a message of wisdom, to another a message of knowledge by means of the same Spirit, to another faith by the same Spirit, to another gifts of healing by that one Spirit." (1 Cor. 12:7-8)

Follow these principles, and your discussion will strengthen what has been proposed by the sub-team!

As for the process, I recommend focusing on each of the objectives prior to considering strategies. Your task, while challenging, is straightforward: For each objective, determine whether you will keep it as proposed, combine it with another objective to make a new objective, change the objective in some way, remove the objective from consideration, or reclassify the objective as a strategy. Additionally, the team may elect to add new objectives to those that have been proposed. *Do not at this point worry about getting to five or less objectives* – we'll cross that bridge soon enough. Rather, shift your focus to strategies, assessing each to determine whether to keep, combine, change, or remove. And of course new strategies may be added to the mix.

PRIORITIZE

Here, as the saying goes, is where the rubber meets the road. Regardless of whether you're already down to five or fewer objectives, and/or five or fewer strategies for each objective, there is a need to prioritize your work.

One of the hardest things for pastors and leaders to do is to say "no" to what is good, and "yes" to what is best. If you are down to seven objectives, getting down to five means saying no to at least two good objectives. If you are already down to five objectives, don't lock them in just yet – you may need to hold off on one or two in order to realize greater success in the others.

The *Faith-Based* tools you have completed to this point can assist you in prioritizing objectives and strategies. In fact, a single question relative to each completed tool helps to bring clarity.

If you have completed the *Spiritual Farming worksheet*, ask:
> Taking into account your climate and roots, are there objectives and/or strategies that exceed the pace of change that the staff, leadership, and congregation can realistically handle?

If you have completed the *Deep and Wide exercise*, ask:
> Which objectives and/or strategies are most likely to bring about an increase in either category (deep, wide)?

If you have completed the *Vision Convergence worksheet*, ask:
> Taking into account the three diagrams (passion, how we see God at work, and gaps), which objectives and/or strategies best align with the overlapping areas?

If you have completed the *S.W.O.T. Analysis*, ask:

> Which objectives and/or strategies are most likely to address the opportunities listed?

If you have completed the *"Here to There" worksheet*, ask:

> Which objectives and/or strategies are most likely to move us from "here to there" in the coming year?

As difficult as it might be to hone in on no more than five objectives supported by no more than five strategies, it is imperative that we do just that. Every church – and every pastor and leader – has finite capacity. Our plans must move us toward our mission, but working on too many things at the same time has the opposite effect.

One of the annual planning tools provided in the Key Tools section is the "Solid-Slushy-Liquid" template. This tool is designed to delineate between plans that are "solid" (will do in the coming year), "slushy" (may do in the coming year, but likely to carry into next year), and "liquid" (not likely to undertake in the next few years, but worth holding on to). The tool ensures that objectives and strategies that aren't feasible this year remain on our radar for next year, or the year after.

QUESTIONS FOR DISCUSSION & REFLECTION

• What can we learn about deliberation from the Apostle Paul?

• How can deliberation unite, rather than divide, leaders?

• Why is prioritization critical for annual planning? What are the dangers of not prioritizing well?

14

VALIDATION

**validate: to recognize, establish, or illustrate
the worthiness or legitimacy of**

Congratulations! With the hard work of annual planning behind you, you're ready to perform one last check before locking in your objectives and strategies.

Validation is an important yet often overlooked step in planning. The argument for validation is simple: You've already invested considerable time and energy formulating objectives and strategies, so why not take a few minutes to validate your work before proceeding?

The *F.A.I.T.H. Filter* is a key tool created primarily for validation. The filter lists five essential aspects that plans must pass through before being finalized:

Flexible

Aligned

Intertwined

Transformational

Holy

If you can answer each of the questions below in the affirmative, than you're ready to proceed; if not, take time to discern what changes might need to take place before moving ahead.

Flexible: Are we willing and able to hold our plans loosely, adapting as necessary to the leading of the Holy Spirit?

Aligned: Do our objectives and strategies align with God's call on us? Will they help us be faithful to our mission, step toward our vision, and uphold our values?

Intertwined: Do our objectives and strategies hang together? Do they encapsulate the purposes of the church?

Transformational: Will our objectives and strategies help bring about transformation in people? In our church? In our community?

Holy: Are we ready and willing to surrender our plans to God?

15

CONSECRATION

**consecrate: to declare to be sacred or holy;
set apart for a sacred purpose**

The last step in annual planning is far and away the best step. Now is the time to consecrate – to dedicate – our plans to God. We give thanks to God for His leading and provision, and ask God to bless and prosper our plans so that He alone receives the glory.

In consecrating our plans to the Lord, we acknowledge our own weaknesses and limitations, yet rejoice that God covers us by grace and calls us to join His redemptive work. This truth alone ought to bring us to our knees – just as it did for the Apostle Paul.

In Ephesians 3:14-21, Paul pauses to pray for the Ephesian Christians. And what a prayer it is! The words Paul writes in these eight verses are some of the sweetest words in all of scripture. Among other things, Paul prays that the Ephesians, "may have power, together with all the Lord's holy people, to grasp how wide and long and high and deep is the love of Christ, and to know this love that surpasses knowledge" (Eph. 3:18-19). Yet before his majestic prayer, Paul writes these simple words: "For this reason, I kneel before the Father" (Eph. 3:14).

Why does Paul mention his posture? Because Paul - "chief of sinners" (1 Tim. 1:15) – had no illusions about his own depravity.

Paul knew that to simply be in God's presence was miraculous. So Paul not only kneels before God, he explains why he kneels: "For this reason." Paul's *reason* is given in the verses just prior:

> "I became a servant of this gospel by the gift of God's grace given me through the working of his power. Although I am less than the least of all the Lord's people, this grace was given me: to preach to the Gentiles the boundless riches of Christ, and to make plain to everyone the administration of this mystery, which for ages past was kept hidden in God, who created all things. His intent was that now, through the church, the manifold wisdom of God should be made known to the rulers and authorities in the heavenly realms, according to his eternal purpose that he accomplished in Christ Jesus our Lord." (Eph. 3:7-11)

How's that for a reason! In verse 7, Paul received the grace of God; in verse 8, Paul is called by God to preach the Gospel to the Gentiles; in verse 9, Paul is made aware that this Gospel he'll be preaching is central to God's plan of redemption; and in verses 10-11, Paul reveals God's plan that the church will be the means by which God will be made known. Paul had ample reason to kneel before the Father. May the same be said about us!

PART FIVE

ALIGNMENT

There was a television commercial some years back where a man is on the phone with his boss, and as the boss barks at him non-stop, every few seconds the man confidently interjects with, "I can do that." When the call ends, the man turns with a dazed look on his face and mutters to himself, "How am I going to do that?"

The *Alignment* phase of strategic planning can feel that way. The big dreams that accompany long-range planning, and the energy and anticipation that come with annual planning, give way to the difficult challenge of aligning ministries, departments, staff, and finances to the strategic plan. In the Alignment phase, "we can do that" assurance is shrouded by "how are we going to do that?" reality.

In my experience, the alignment phase is often the most challenging of all in that it typically necessitates difficult decisions and painful adjustments. Yet misalignment is the single biggest reason that well discerned, well formed strategic plans don't bear fruit. And when I state that this is my experience, I mean just that – there have been planning seasons when I was not adamant or courageous enough to align key resources with objectives and strategies, and in those seasons I hurt the church.

The hard truth is that alignment requires change, and change is usually painful – especially as it relates to ministries, departments, governance, staff members, and budgets. But without proper alignment, trying to realize objectives and strategies is like trying to paddle a canoe upstream. With hard work, there can be forward movement, but it is slow and unsustainable.

The Alignment phase is focused primarily on three areas: ministries/departments, organizational structure (staffing and governance), and general budget. Each of these must support and help bring attainment to the overarching elements of mission, vision, values, objectives and strategies. Alignment is easy to grasp but hard to attain. Many churches are open to seeking the Holy Spirit's leading, but few are willing to follow the Spirit's leading all the way through.

Think back to the Deliberation chapter in the preceding section. We imagined a church that discerned an objective to "Enhance the overall worship experience," supported by two strategies: to "Enhance the worship environment," and to "Alter the worship style." Most certainly, to achieve the objective the church would need to align its resources to the objective. They would need to consider contracting with an outside consultant to help guide them through sound, light, and aesthetic changes. They would need to consider the gifts and talents needed by staff and key volunteers to support the new worship style. And they would need to consider whether the current worship director is the right person to lead in this capacity going forward. They would need to consider all of this and more.

But what happens if the worship director begins to speak out against the proposed changes, and rallies others to her side? What happens if the church treasurer insists that the church cannot, under any circumstances, take on a budget increase? What happens if a staff member tells his volunteers that he does not agree with what has been proposed, and that he may need to resign? What happens if congregants threaten to withhold giving, or to leave the church, if this crazy talk of change doesn't stop?

I have experienced all of this and more. Chances are you have too. And to be fair, sometimes resistance to change is reasonable and warranted – if there is an honest belief that the proposed changes will diminish the church's witness and ability to make disciples. But most often, resistance to change stems not from concern for the Gospel, but fear and self-interests.

This is why it's so important for church leaders to stand in the gap and see change through, even when it affects ministries, departments, staff members, and budgets. And yes, even when people threaten to withhold giving or to leave the church. When others are mired in fear and consumed by self-interest, leaders must remain rooted in faith and driven by the advance of the Gospel.

DISMANTLING TOWERS

When a pastor, or staff member, or ministry, or department, or governing board, work against the grain of the church's mission, vision, and objectives, they build a tower unto themselves. The principle comes from Genesis 11:

> "Now the whole world had one language and a common speech. As people moved eastward, they found a plain in Shinar and settled there. They said to each other, 'Come, let's make bricks and bake them thoroughly.' They used brick instead of stone, and tar for mortar. Then they said, 'Come, let us build ourselves a city, with a tower that reaches to the heavens, so that we may make a name for ourselves; otherwise we will be scattered over the face of the whole earth.'" (Genesis 11:1-4)

Think of it. This large assembly of people gathered in Shinar and shared the misguided notion that on their own strength, independent of God, they might actually ascend beyond human limitation and to the very threshold of the divine - "to the heavens." Is this not the epitome of delusion? A tower to the heavens, really? How high do you have to build that sort of tower?

It begs a fundamental question: What could possibly have moved the people in Shinar to take on this misguided building project?

The answer, in a word, is pride. Verse 2 states that, "As people moved eastward, they found a plain in Shinar and settled there." The statement may seem innocuous, but upon closer examination it's anything but.

Historians estimate that the Tower of Babel was built around 2200 BC, which means it would have been built around 100 years after the flood. They believe this to be the case in part because Nimrod was known to be the leader of the group that settled in Shinar and built the tower, and Nimrod was the son of Cush, who was the son of Ham, who was the son of Noah. All of this matters because of what Scripture records in Genesis 9:1, that God blessed Noah and his sons, and instructed them to "Be fruitful and increase in number and fill the earth."

In the space of a mere hundred years or so, and spanning just a couple of generations, the command of God to "be fruitful and increase in number and fill the earth" was blatantly rejected. The people moved eastward, found themselves a nice plain in Shinar, and decided that they would stay right there, thank you very much. They were blatantly disobedient, and at the root of their disobedience was pride, which becomes clearer still in verse 4:

> "Let us build ourselves a city, with a tower that reaches to the heavens, so that we may make a name for ourselves; otherwise we will be scattered over the face of the earth."

Talk about arrogance! The people rebelled against God by settling in Shinar, and to make matters worse they set out to build a city – not for the glory of God, but for their own glory: "Let us build *ourselves* a city." But wait, there's more! This city wasn't going to be just any city, this city would have a majestic tower that would reach clear to the heavens, to the threshold of the divine. Why? So that they might make a name for themselves. The people in Shinar were so overcome with pride that they couldn't grasp reality. That's the effect pride has on people.

In *Mere Christianity*, C.S. Lewis described the problem of pride this way: "Pride is spiritual cancer: it eats up the very possibility of love, or contentment, or even common sense." [22]

That's what was happening in Shinar. The people were so stricken with this spiritual cancer called pride that they were unable to love, or be content, or even think straight.

It's tempting to dismiss what took place in Shinar as an ancient, humorous little blooper reel in the long history of human bloopers. But let's be honest. When we give into pride, we do exactly what the people in Shinar did – we build towers. Not towers of brick and mortar, but towers of isolation, achievement, elitism, recognition.

When a ministry or staff member or governing board functions in isolation, they build a tower. When they point time and time again to all of the good things *they* have done, they build a tower. When they work not with others but against others, they build a tower. When they are consumed with praise and recognition, they build a tower.

And so we are clear, tower building is ultimately a leadership issue. As the leader goes, so goes the ministry (or department, governing board, staff, etc.). And in the church of Jesus Christ, leadership devoid of followership isn't leadership at all. It's tower construction.

In Shinar, the people were united behind their leader, Nimrod, a man that Scripture informs us was a mighty warrior who stood not with the Lord but before the Lord – *in defiance of the Lord.* Nimrod's very name means "one who rebels." What does this hold for today's church leaders? How about this: *Don't be a Nimrod!*

Sorry, just couldn't resist. But it is true, yes? We all have a choice to make. We can focus on ourselves and build towers, or we can focus on Christ and join Him in building His church.

In fairness, most of us are in fact committed to serving Christ and His church in ministry - yet struggle at times with setting aside our own interests in favor of the greater good. I know this to be true because I have more experience building towers than I care to admit. But I didn't set out to build towers, and I don't believe that the large majority of church leaders do either. Instead, towers get built slowly, steadily, and oftentimes unknowingly.

But here's the good news - there is no tower too big for God to knock down:

> "But the Lord came down to see the city and the tower the people were building. The Lord said, 'If as one people speaking the same language they have begun to do this, then nothing they plan to do will be impossible for them. Come, let us go down and confuse their language so they will not understand each other.' So the Lord scattered them from there over all the earth, and they stopped building the city. That is why it was called Babel - because there the Lord confused the language of the whole world. From

there the Lord scattered them over the face of the whole earth." (Genesis 11:5-9)

God is extraordinarily compassionate! Confusing their language and scattering the people over all the earth was an act of discipline to be sure, but more than that it was an act of unmerited, unfathomable love. God gave the people a mulligan – a do-over – of epic proportion. God put a stop to their building project in order to save them from themselves, and to help them turn back to His plan and purpose for them.

There is no tower too big for God to tear down. If you've built a tower, ask God to tear it down. Fall on your knees, confess your building project to God, and recommit to joining Christ in the work of building His church – the *whole* church.

16

MINISTRY/DEPARTMENT PLANS

Ministry/Department Plans are typically set by staff members, and answer the question of how ministries and departments, in the coming year, will help fulfill the mission, step toward the vision, and support the objectives and strategies.

Before considering how to go about formulating ministry/department plans, we must first identify which ministries and departments to include. My recommendation is to include all *primary* ministries and departments, but not *sub-ministries/departments* or programs. For example, the children's ministry as a whole should be included, but nursery, Children's Sunday school, and children's midweek programs should not. This is not to diminish the importance of these ministries and programs, but to point out that they are best considered in the broader context of children's ministry as a whole.

Be sure to include primary ministries and departments that fall directly under one of the five purposes. If you have a missions/outreach team, or an adult discipleship ministry, or a worship ministry, include them in your listing of ministries and departments.

ALIGNMENT

It is important for each ministry and department to verify their alignment with the mission first, and with newly established objectives second.

Every ministry and department must exist to help enable the disciple-making mission of the church. The buildings & grounds department does not exist to maintain the building and grounds, but to maintain the building and grounds so that the church can live out its mission. The office & administration department does not exist to carry out the business functions of the church, but to carry out the business functions of the church so that the church is able to carry out its mission. All ministries and departments exist to support and enable the mission.

Yet it is not at all uncommon for church ministries and departments to narrow their focus so much that instead of supporting the mission, they stifle the mission. The buildings and grounds department can become so consumed with cleanliness that the building becomes a "look but don't touch" museum rather than a "come as you are" place of grace and hospitality. The church administrator can become so focused on protocol and procedure that he ends up being a gatekeeper rather than a gateway. Even ministries for children and youth, with a clear charter to disciple young people, can become misaligned with the mission if fun and games become a higher priority than biblical teaching and sound doctrine.

This is why before ministries and departments work to align plans with objectives and strategies, they must first, with honesty and humility, consider their alignment with the mission. For ministries and departments that have strayed far, this may necessitate significant adjustment. But for ministries and departments that are diligent to keep the church's mission as their mission, fine tuning is sufficient to realign with the mission.

Bearing in mind that our mission is both wide *("go")* and deep *("make disciples")*, here are a few suggestions to help ministries and departments align well with the mission:

To get wider ...

Use the Two-Degree Rule.
This suggestion comes courtesy of pastor and author Kevin G. Harney, who in his *Organic Outreach* series provides a number of easy to implement, highly effective approaches for naturally, organically reaching people for Christ. One of the approaches Kevin gives is the Two-Degree Rule, which he describes as, "the concept that we can intentionally push the needle of the church a couple of degrees off dead north and vector some of our resources, time, care, energy and love toward those who are in the community and still far from God ... you are not looking at starting new ministries with new volunteers and additional resources. You are simply taking what you are doing well and extending it past your 'Jerusalem' and into your community."[23]

Take a walk.
Very few pastors and ministry/department leaders carve out regular times to walk around and pray over their community. Fewer still do so as a whole ministry or

department team. Yet there is no question that a willingness to "go" and pray for people and homes in your neighborhood will help align your ministry or department to the mission you are called to. Prayer walking is a surefire way to recalibrate and refocus.

Have your ministry or department join together in regular mission or service projects.
Every community has needs that can be met by volunteer groups. Whether it's serving in a soup kitchen or homeless shelter, helping at a local school, or taking a short-term mission trip together, ministry and department teams align better with their mission when they intentionally step into the mission. But don't do this once and check the box! Rather, plan something regularly, be it monthly, quarterly, or every six months.

To get deeper ...

Start ministry or department meetings with prayer and teaching.
The health and vitality of ministries and departments is tied to how the leader leads regular meetings. Ministry and department meetings are built-in opportunities to teach, encourage, challenge, and pray together. Creating a culture of deep discipleship starts with leaders, and there is no excuse for not allowing ample time in meetings for prayer and learning. And if you really want to grow leaders, have team members take turns teaching and leading prayer.

Be a mentor, find a mentor.

What would the health of your ministry or department be if its leaders and key volunteers were both mentoring someone and being mentored themselves? I have had the joy of being both a mentor and mentee, and can say with conviction that both are catalysts for spiritual growth. But more than that, mentoring creates a pronounced ripple effect - when one person is transformed, others are effected too. As leaders and volunteers in ministries and departments grow, so too does their understanding of what they are called to do, individually and as a team.

Be active in another ministry.

I have met with many pastors and ministry leaders who are not involved in a ministry outside of their own. This, I believe, is a mistake. Leading a ministry can take a heavy toll on a person, and cause faithful leaders to spend all of their energy and focus on their own ministry. People are more rounded and ultimately better equipped to serve and lead effectively when they participate (but don't lead) in a ministry outside of their assigned area of responsibility, and possibly even outside of their own church. I realize that this is difficult given the demands of ministry, but your spiritual health, and the spiritual health of the ministry or department you lead, depend on you doing so.

After alignment with the mission comes alignment with objectives and strategies. Is this important? Vitally so!

Imagine a professional football team whose mission, year in and year out, is to win a championship. The mission drives the front office to work tirelessly scouting, drafting, and trading for players that they believe have what it takes to achieve the mission. Every season the coaches work to implement offensive and defensive plans that they believe give their team the best chance to win. During the season, a specific game plan is developed for each opponent. And in the course of each game, numerous adjustments are made.

In football, to compete for a championship, there must be strong alignment throughout, from ownership to coaches to players, and all points in between. Agreement on the mission – to relentlessly pursue a championship - is a great start. But if there isn't agreement on *how* to pursue a championship, the team is in big trouble. For example, if the general manager drafts big, powerful offensive linemen built to excel in a run-heavy offense, and the offensive coordinator plans for an up tempo, pass-heavy offense, the offense will be out of sync and unproductive.

Losing teams almost always lack cohesion. Not so with winning teams, who not only commit fully to the mission but actively support and align with overarching plans. It's true in football, and it's true in the church. But while alignment to mission and objectives is essential, so too is safeguarding the primary function of each ministry and department. It is possible to over-align with an objective such that a ministry or department loses sight of its unique place, its unique function, in the church. Navigating through how best to support a church-wide objective while safeguarding the primary function of a ministry or department requires discernment, dialogue, and adjustment.

A few years ago Remembrance Church discerned an objective to create and launch a second worship service that we believed would appeal to unreached and de-churched people in our community. It was subsequently determined that the start time for the existing first service would remain at 9:30 a.m., with the new service starting at 11:00 a.m. And it was further determined that the discipleship hour, when classes were available to people of all ages, would take place between 11:00 a.m. and noon.

With key details in place, it was time for our ministries and departments to align with the objective. For some, alignment necessitated significant adjustment; for others, very little. In all cases, the challenge was to support and align with the objective while at the same time safeguarding the primary function of the ministry or department. Hence...

- ✓ The Office & Administration department developed a plan to incorporate the new service into a single worship bulletin, rather than publish two separate bulletins;
- ✓ The Buildings & Grounds department developed a plan to alter the seating arrangement between services in order to give the second service a more intimate setting;
- ✓ The Board of Deacons changed their approach to collecting and counting;
- ✓ The Board of Elders pledged to support the new service through direct participation, including being present for post-service prayer opportunities;
- ✓ The Care ministry refined Guest Services to better accommodate the new service;
- ✓ The Discipleship & Small Groups ministry worked to plug new visitors into LIFE Groups;
- ✓ The Outreach ministry pledged to invite people in the community to the new service;
- ✓ The Children's ministry, and Youth ministry, altered their Sunday schedules to align with the discipleship hour.

To varying degrees, all ministries and departments made changes to support the new service! But as is so often the case, our plans needed significant adjustment throughout the season and beyond. In fact, shortly after the new service launched, we realized that we had missed the mark in several areas, not the least of which was not having youth in the service, since they were taking part in the discipleship hour.

What happened next is a testimony to the value of strong leadership and willing collaboration. With a desire to support the new worship service, and with a responsibility to effectively disciple students, our youth director created a plan to allow students to attend the first service, and the first fifteen minutes of the second service, before leaving as a group for the discipleship hour, which for them would extend to 12:15 p.m. The plan created inconvenience, but it served to align the ministry with the objective, while safeguarding the primary function of the ministry.

Over the next few years, additional adjustments were made, and continue to be made. Adding the new service has been a challenge for Remembrance, but they have persevered, and have received the Lord's blessing through many new believers and two vibrant worship services. [24]

ESTABLISHING MINISTRY/DEPARTMENT PLANS

Unlike objectives and strategies that are discerned through broad leadership collaboration, ministry and department plans are discerned largely by ministry and department leaders, who most often are staff members. Collaboration with volunteers and other staff members is important, but ultimately the leader, who is called, gifted, and equipped to lead the ministry or department, must put her stamp of approval on plans.

For many years, I have employed a "Keep-Alter-Stop-Add" process to help leaders discern ministry and department plans. The approach is simple but effective. To get started, use the template provided as a key tool, and follow the steps below:

1. *Take inventory.*

    List all existing sub-ministries/departments, programs, and regular activities and events. This list should encompass the large majority of what the ministry or department does, and where its budgeted funds are allocated.

2. *Selectively add ideas generated during ideation.*

    Review the list of ideas that were generated during ideation. If there are ideas pertaining to your ministry or department that you believe have merit, list them in the 'Ideas' section.

3. *Classify sub-ministries, programs, and regular activities and events (Keep, Alter, Stop).*

    Taking into account the church-wide objectives and strategies, and being careful to safeguard the primary function of your ministry or department, classify each existing sub-ministry, program, and regular activity/event.

Under 'Keep', list sub-ministries, programs and regular activities/events that are already effective and require no adjustment. Verify that each item listed serves the primary function of the ministry/department and/or aligns with a given objective or strategy.

Under 'Alter', list sub-ministries, programs and regular activities/events that need to be changed in order to better serve the primary function of the ministry/department, or to align with a given objective or strategy. Give a brief explanation of the change.

Under 'Stop', list sub-ministries, programs and regular activities/events that no longer effectively serve the primary function of the ministry/department, or are misaligned with a given objective or strategy. Give a brief explanation for the decision to stop.

4. *Selectively consider what to add.*

As a general rule, I recommend that for every sub-ministry, program or activity/event added, another should be stopped. My rationale is simple: the large majority of churches, and church leaders, are already functioning at capacity. Layering on more "stuff" may seem wise, but most often it results in mission distraction, along with frustrated leaders and members.

That said, in nearly every planning season there emerges a need to add to (and subtract from) the mix.

New objectives create new needs, most of which are met by altering what is done currently, but in some cases necessitating something new altogether. And every new season requires realignment to the mission, and optimization of ministry or department effectiveness, which may surface the need for new offerings.

5. *Project the budget impact.*

Taking into account what you are proposing to keep, alter, stop, and add, list the projected impact to the budget. Resist the temptation to understate cost in order to present a best case scenario, or to overstate cost to present a worst-case scenario. Rather, do your best to project the most likely scenario for each item listed.

6. *Refine the plan with your supervisor, and present it to the staff.*

I am a strong proponent of staff leaders collaborating with their immediate supervisor prior to releasing ministry/department plans. When senior leaders have a clear understanding of how ministry or department plans align with the mission, support the objectives, and optimize the ministry/department, they are able to endorse and actively support plans in credible fashion. Additionally, I have found it to be tremendously helpful when staff leaders share their plans with one another. I recommend allocating at least two hours for this important activity. The encouragement, synergy and cohesiveness that emerges when ministry/department plans are presented is a blessing to all. A good wrap-up to this meeting is to walk through the F.A.I.T.H. Filter as a staff, pledging support to one another while affirming that our individual plans hold together as a single, unified plan.

QUESTIONS FOR DISCUSSION & REFLECTION

- How might your ministry or department better align with the mission? Would any of the "deep" or "wide" ideas listed help bring about stronger alignment with the mission?

- Describe the primary function of your ministry or department.

- How has your church done in the past with having all ministries and departments support key initiatives or objectives? How might you improve in this area going forward?

17

STAFFING AND GOVERNANCE

A long time ago in a workforce far, far away, I began my post-college working career. Using cutting edge technology like Lotus Word Pro on a Commodore 128, I was able to create, print, photocopy, and distribute memos through an intricate interoffice mail system. I used a fax machine that worked a good 60% of the time – not bad! Along with just about everyone else in corporate America, I read *In Search of Excellence* by Tom Peters, a book offering terrific insights from America's best run companies.[25] And I figured that if I worked hard enough, someday I might be trusted with a gigantic mobile phone, the kind that only high ranking executives and outside sales people seemed to carry.

Stating the obvious, in the thirty years since I began my career, incredible advances in technology have dramatically changed how we work, and how we live. What was cutting edge thirty years ago, or even ten years ago, is ancient history today. What is cutting edge today will be an answer to a trivia question tomorrow. Whether we like it or not, our rapidly changing world forces us to make a choice: adapt or isolate. And as church leaders we must choose wisely, because the stakes could not be higher.

Our reality is this: Thriving churches are those whose leaders willingly adapt to a changing world, yet remain rooted in, and driven by, their mission. These leaders see no dissonance between safeguarding an unchanging Gospel and adapting to an ever-changing world. Like Paul, they willingly become all things to all people so that by all possible means they might win some – *for the sake of the Gospel* (1 Cor. 9:22-23).

But there is another reality to acknowledge, which is that most church leaders (and churches) struggle with safeguarding the Gospel and adapting to the culture. It's not easy to do, and if the struggle is honest, leaders and churches deserve commendation for at least striving to do both. On the other hand, many church leaders, and many churches, have no interest whatsoever in combining Gospel stewardship with cultural adaptability. Their preference is to either isolate themselves from the culture, giving them no ability to speak into the culture, or assimilate to the culture, resulting in sameness rather than set apartness.

In the latter case, we must make a clear distinction between adapting to the world and assimilating to the world. Adaptation helps us to understand and minister with relevance to a broken world. Assimilation, however, conforms us to the world. To adapt is to be in the world; to assimilate is to be of the world. Paul exemplifies the difference in that everywhere he traveled, he acknowledged but did not partake in the surrounding culture. Today's church leaders must do the same, adapting their ministry to reach the culture, and sharing the good news of Jesus Christ in all places and at all times.

STAFFING

The ability of your church to fulfill the mission, step toward the vision, live out values, and carry out annual plans rests heavily on your church staff. Structuring for alignment and attainment of key priorities is critical, yet often overlooked in churches. So too is working to ensure that staff members are equipped, empowered, and appreciated. Simply put, the church functions at its best when healthy, fulfilled leaders serve in roles that tap into their unique passions, gifts and strengths.

Structuring for Success

By way of confession, I have been a fan of the Detroit Lions football team for as long as I can remember. Cut me open, and I bleed Honolulu blue! For over four decades, I have watched this team vacillate between mediocrity and abject failure, with a smattering of success sprinkled in (but not much – just one playoff win in my lifetime!). Over the years, the Lions have changed general managers, hired new coaches, and overhauled their roster numerous times, but have little to show for it. And while I am just a fan who has no knowledge of the inner workings of their front office, from the outside it certainly appears that what has plagued the Lions more than anything is a failure to establish and commit to an identity, and to build a team that reflects who they desire to be.

The Lions represent a stark contrast to successful teams like the Pittsburgh Steelers and New England Patriots, who do have an identity, and who hire coaches and players that fit their system and perpetuate success. Perhaps the most telling comparison is this: In the fifteen seasons between 2000 and 2014, the Steelers had two head coaches, the Patriots one head coach, and the Lions eight head coaches. Not coincidentally, in that same span, the Steelers had nine playoff appearances with two Super Bowl victories, the Patriots twelve playoff appearances with four Super Bowl victories, and the Lions two playoff appearances, both losses.

Losing teams lack identity. Winning teams – and winning churches - know who they are, and remain steadfast in building a team that reflects who they are. Values are protected and passed on by committed leaders who know what, and who, they stand for. History and tradition are important, but not nearly as important as the mission that convicts them, and the vision that compels them. And winning churches understand the need to align their staff with how the Holy Spirit is leading the church.

In every planning season, senior leaders must objectively assess whether the current staffing structure and makeup supports the church's mission, vision, values, and plans. This can be difficult, even painful work. Frankly, its work that I have shied away from throughout most of my career, as I've held the misguided notion that aligning staff to a strategic plan is healthy for an organization but harmful to individuals. It is only recently that I have come to realize that when plans are carefully, prayerfully discerned, aligning staff with how the Holy Spirit leads benefits not only the church, but people - including those who are redeployed or released.

To trust in the Lord with all of our heart, and to lean not on our own understanding, is to cast aside our preconceived notions of what we think will happen to people if they are asked to assume a different role, or are released from the church altogether. To be faith-based is to act in accordance with God's leading rather than what we want. I have yet to meet a leader who enjoys releasing staff members, but I respect leaders who with courage and faith do what they must do rather than what they prefer to do.

Ultimately, the question is one of trust: If God has set a plan before the church, and the plan necessitates changes to the staff, do we trust that the God who is leading the church into something new might also be leading people into something new?

God's plans for churches are not incompatible with His plans for people. God causes *all things* to work together for good to those who love Him, who have been called according to His purpose (Romans 8:28).

As mentioned, I have been slow to embrace this truth, and for that I sincerely repent. And God has been gracious to show me that His plans for people are ultimately what's best for them. In fact, every person I have had to release during my ministry career has emerged better for it, if not immediately most definitely in the long run. And I have experienced this in my own life as well.

Fifteen months prior to the time of this writing, and with the blessing of the church I was serving at the time, I transitioned from full-time to half-time as the church's administrative pastor, and in parallel accepted a half-time position to lead a classis of eighteen churches. Around a year later, I was informed that my half-time role at the church would be reverting back to full-time. I found myself at a crossroad that I didn't see coming. I sensed God calling me to stay in the half-time classis role, but longed for the security of full-time employment. After a time of prayer, soul searching, and counsel with others, I resigned from the church so that they could proactively begin searching for my replacement. Subsequently, and in short order, God's plan for me materialized when I was presented with an opportunity to work half-time for our regional synod, in a capacity that would ideally complement my existing classis role. God had a plan for the church, and the classis, and the region, and myself – a plan that strengthened each, and a plan with no incompatibility whatsoever.

As you seek to align your staff with the strategic plan, here are some questions to consider:

Do the staff positions of the church align with and support the priorities (mission, vision, values, objectives, strategies) of the church?

As the church sets a new direction, it is not uncommon for roles that were once vital to have less significance going forward. It is also not uncommon for new needs to emerge as a result of a new direction. Senior leaders must consider staffing needs in light of what must be, rather than what has been.

If changes are necessary, are there people on your staff who can thrive in a new role?

In some cases, existing staff members have it in them to transition to, and excel in, a new role. But exercise caution, being careful not to make a bad decision out of emotion, or to "do right" by a staff member. Seek to discern as best you can whether the staff member is truly excited about the change, or just looking for a place to land.

Do staff members differentiate between primary and secondary aspects of their roles?

Before adding staff or changing responsibilities, verify that staff members are able to differentiate and prioritize primary from secondary job aspects. As one day blends with the next, and as new crises emerge, it is easy for staff members to lose sight of the most critical aspects of their role. Fortunately, in most cases the staff member simply needs to be reminded and redirected. But in some cases, particularly when a staff member's priorities don't align with the church's priorities, it may be best to part ways.

Does your staffing plan align with the general budget?
Recent studies suggest that churches should allocate 45%-55% of the total budget for human resource expenses.[26] While the range is intended strictly as a guideline, I have found it to be reasonable and helpful. I encourage you to calculate the human resource allocation of the overall church budget, and consider its effect on the church's ability to meet its strategic plan. An understaffed church will not be able to lead a far-reaching plan, and an overstaffed church will likely lack the ability to invest in key ministry and missional priorities.

Does your hiring process align with your priorities?
When considering adding staff, make sure that the proposed role, be it existing or new, aligns with and supports the priorities of the church. Where it makes sense, consider alternatives to adding new staff members (oftentimes, existing staff members or key volunteers are the best choice to meet the need). If you decide to initiate a search, begin with this premise: Do not, *ever*, compromise your mission, vision, and values by hiring someone just to fill a chair. Conduct your search as if the advance of the Gospel depends on it! Because whether your church is a mega church or a mini church, it is a church of Jesus Christ. That alone is reason enough to hire staff members who

embrace their identity in Christ, align with the values of the church, and commit wholeheartedly to advancing the Gospel of Jesus Christ.

Strengthening for Sustainability

Staff turnover is to be expected, and ought to be celebrated when healthy churches grow and bless healthy leaders who obediently follow where God calls. But far too frequently, staff departures are prompted not by a fresh call, but mounting frustration. As leaders, our responsibility does not end with getting the right people in the right seats. We must also be intentional to equip, empower, and encourage our staff on an ongoing basis.

Equipping Staff

A soldier is not sent to battle without proper training. A firefighter cannot subdue a fire without proper equipment. An athlete will not excel without practice. Yet church workers are routinely sent to the front lines of ministry without proper training, or tools, or practice.

One sure way to demoralize staff members is to expect them to excel in their role without being adequately equipped. And to be clear, adequate equipping does not happen at a point in time, but on an ongoing basis. A degree or program of study is essential for preparation, but sustained excellence requires continued learning and growth.

Healthy churches understand that encouraging and assisting staff members to grow is not a burden, but an investment. But staff members must be willing to grow, understanding that sustained high performance comes only through sustained learning. Church leaders and staff members must each do their part; stagnation is not an option for the church of Jesus Christ.

Beyond growth opportunities, staff members must be provided with the necessary tools and equipment needed to function in their roles. Desktop computers do not help staff members who do a portion of their work from home. Antiquated computers running Windows 95 don't help anyone! For staff members to excel, they must have the right tools and equipment.

Finally, give your staff opportunities to practice, and to stretch out. During my ministry career, I have been blessed to witness a building and grounds director start a ministry for ex-offenders, an administrative assistant lead a missions committee, and a youth pastor start a new worship service. I could continue but you get the point. Each of these people made a point of practicing, of stretching out, to prepare for what the Lord had in store.

Empowering Staff

The single biggest investment churches make is in staff. However, for many churches, the financial investment is not matched by a willingness to empower staff to lead the church. Oftentimes, the reluctance to empower staff stems from senior leaders being uneasy about relinquishing control and influence. In some cases, their concern is well founded and necessary to protect the church from a rogue or misguided staff member. But if the desire to control is widespread rather than situational, the staff will never step into its full potential, and the church will suffer as a result.

For leaders who struggle with giving up control, the journey from stifling to empowering staff is exceedingly difficult. Deeply embedded mental models and long standing behavioral patterns don't change overnight. And the root of the issue is not a lack of trust in people, but a lack of trust in God. Yet for the person who repents and invites God to change his heart and renew his mind, there is hope – not through blind determination, but through the God who is able to do immeasurably more than we ask or imagine.

Encouraging Staff

Ministry is not for the faint of heart! While there are numerous blessings that come from serving the Lord and His people, so too are there numerous challenges - many of which are very, very messy. In the absence of encouragement, the best church workers can hope for is to hang in and survive. But with regular encouragement, church workers are positioned to thrive.

Encouragement comes both from God, who is our strength and shield (Psalm 28:7), and from God's people, who are to encourage and build one another up (1 Thes. 5:11).

We know that God will do His part if only we seek Him (Psalm 121). But what about us? How are we to encourage and build up our staff? The list that follows represents a good start:

Be Present.
So often in ministry, church workers feel isolated and alone. Being present with staff members – checking in on them, asking how they are doing, praying for them – can make all the difference.

Affirm staff members.
In my ministry, I have the privilege of connecting with many pastors and leaders. I am blessed to share in their joys and humbled to share in their sorrows. What saddens

me more than anything is when a pastor or leader does not feel affirmed. How easy it is to forget that all people need affirmation. I'm not suggesting that we flatter staff members to boost their self-confidence, but that we sincerely and honestly let them know they are appreciated. Just as people must *hear* the Gospel to respond to it (Romans 10:14), so too must people hear words of affirmation to feel affirmed.

Compensate staff members fairly.

Scripture makes clear that those whose vocational work is the spread of the Gospel are to be paid fairly for their work. When Jesus sent the seventy-two out, He told them to eat and drink what was offered to them, "for the worker deserves his wages" (Luke 10:7). Paul made several mentions of the need for church workers to be compensated fairly (Romans 4:4, 1 Cor.9:9-14, 2 Cor. 11:7-9, Phil. 4:16-19, 2 Thes. 3:7-10, 1 Tim. 5:17-18). Churches must consider their size, viability, financial health, and denominational policy when establishing fair standards for staff compensation. External wage surveys are helpful if they include data from comparably sized churches in the same region. As you consider total compensation, be sure to account for health and ancillary insurance premiums, as well as retirement contribution. Additionally, churches should plan for an annual cost of living allowance (COLA).

Establish and commit to an annual employee evaluation process.

There has been considerable debate during the past several years over whether performance evaluations help or hinder employee performance. But in my experience, I have found that most staff members, especially those who are driven to excel, clamor for a formal performance evaluation. Still, while I have used an evaluation process for several years, I only recommend giving annual performance evaluations if the church's senior leaders endorse doing so, and if the evaluation process is geared to build up rather than tear down staff members. I believe that a good evaluation process accentuates strengths, identifies areas for improvement, and creates an opportunity for a supervisor and staff member to collaborate on a development plan.

GOVERNANCE

Governing leaders serve a vital purpose in the church of Jesus Christ. In fact, I would go so far as to say that other than the lead pastor, elders and deacons are positioned to exert the most influence in the church. Jesus taught that, "from everyone who has been given much, much will be demanded." This lesson is one that every elder and deacon ought to take to heart! Their positions are a high calling. And the privilege of leading in Christ's church comes with the expectation that leaders follow where God leads. Governing leaders must embrace, embody, and help enable their church's mission, vision, values, and plans.

The influence of elders and deacons cannot be overstated. Over the past several years, as I've worked with many governing leaders and boards, I have seen most work diligently to enable the church to advance, but others that have worked just as diligently to restrict the church from advancing. Some leaders and boards are instruments, others are obstacles. This is why it's critical for churches to do all they can to ensure that those who serve in key leadership roles are of strong character, desiring to enable rather than control the church.

Based on 1 Timothy 3:1-10 and Titus 1:5-9, Pastor Eric Cook of Remembrance Church lists sixteen vital characteristics for governing leaders:

- ✓ A desire to serve - a heart set on serving.
- ✓ Above reproach – no offensive character or conduct.
- ✓ One spouse – purity in marital and sexual life.
- ✓ Temperate – displaying mental sobriety and stability.
- ✓ Self-controlled – prudent, exercising good judgment and common sense.
- ✓ Respectable – well behaved and orderly.
- ✓ Hospitable – offering a concrete expression of Christian love and family life.
- ✓ Able to Teach – able to guide and protect the church by understanding and instructing from the Bible.
- ✓ Not addicted to alcohol (or drugs, gambling, etc. – free from addiction).
- ✓ Not violent – not hot-tempered or irritable.
- ✓ Gentle – kind, quick to display empathy toward others.
- ✓ Not quarrelsome – peaceable rather than divisive.
- ✓ Free from love of money – not greedy, won't use ministry for personal gain.
- ✓ Manages household well – if married, a responsible spouse; if a parent, a responsible parent.
- ✓ Not a recent convert – fully devoted and deeply rooted.
- ✓ Good reputation with outsiders – the church's witness is tied to the moral reputation of its leaders.

If the list seems stringent, that's because it's supposed to be! Leadership in the church is not a right, but a privilege. Too many churches make the mistake of bringing people into leadership roles that they have no business occupying. Is it not better to have a smaller governing board made up of leaders who possess these characteristics than a larger board watered down by people who don't?

Hebrews 13:7 says to, "Remember your leaders, who spoke the word of God to you. Consider the outcome of their way of life and imitate their faith." Be selective when considering potential leaders! Your elders and deacons must be rooted in faith and worthy of imitation.

QUESTIONS FOR DISCUSSION & REFLECTION

- Does your staffing model and makeup allow you to achieve the objectives and strategies you have discerned?

- Does your staff receive regular encouragement? What impact does encouragement have on staff member performance?

- In what ways do you assess and vet prospective elders and deacons?

18

BUDGET AND MINISTRY PLAN

"For where your treasure is, there your heart will be also."
Matthew 6:21

It has been said that to discover a person's priorities, just look through their checkbook. And we know this to be true, don't we? How and where we spend our money reveals our priorities. The same is true for churches: To discover a church's priorities, just examine their budget. A budget with little or no provision for missions and outreach reveals a church that is likely focused more on themselves than others. A budget with little or no provision for discipleship reveals a church that has likely lost its zeal to make disciples. A budget with a disproportionately high (over 60%) investment in personnel reveals a church that likely struggles to identify, develop and mobilize leaders. Conversely, a budget with a disproportionately low investment in personnel (less than 40%) reveals a church that has likely settled for "good enough," and rarely ventures beyond its comfort zone. Where a church's budget is, so too is their heart.

LESSONS FROM THE PARABLE OF THE TALENTS

The Parable of the Talents has been used for generations as a foundational stewardship lesson for individuals. But this same parable offers significant insight for church leaders, leadership boards, and congregations. Fundamentally, the parable challenges us to grapple with how well we know the Master (Jesus), and how we respond to what we know – or what we think we know. The parable gets at the very heart of our life in Christ, individually and corporately. And in the latter case, it is not an exaggeration to point out that the heart of a church almost always reflects how its leaders understand and respond to God.

Take a moment to read Matthew 25:14-30. Read it slowly, letting it wash over you, as you invite the Holy Spirit to minister to you by illuminating God's Word.

∞∞

Let us now consider what the parable holds for us. Significantly, Jesus begins by establishing the Master's character, namely that He is trusting, generous, and wise:

> "For it is as if a man, going on a journey, summoned his slaves and entrusted his property to them; to one he gave five talents, to another two, to another one, each according to his ability. Then he went away." (Matthew 25:14-15)

The Master entrusted the servants with his property, just as God entrusts us with all that He provides - which is, of course, everything (Psalm 24:1). All that the church has – people, finances, buildings, property - belongs to God. The Master is trusting.

And the Master is generous. While there is disparity in what is given to each of the servants, each received a bounty. Max Lucado writes that, "A 'talent' represented the largest unit of accounting in the Greek currency – 10,000 denarii. A denarius represented a day's fair wages (Matt. 20:2). Multiply your daily wage by 10,000, and you discover the value of a talent. If you earn $30,000 a year and work 260 days, a talent in your case is valued at 10,000 times $115 or $1,150,000." [27]

Every church receives abundant blessing and provision from God – sometimes financially, sometimes through other means. We may fret about not having enough, but God is faithful to provide what we need, when we need it. The Master is generous.

And wise. The Master gave different amounts to each servant *according to their ability*. We may think we know what our church needs, but only God knows what we can or can't handle at a given point in time. The Master is wise.

With the Master's character established, Jesus then describes how each servant responds to the Master. Interestingly, while there are three servants, there are but two responses: "Wicked and lazy" (the third servant) and "good and faithful" (the first two servants). Each response is telling and instructive.

Let us first consider what makes for a wicked, lazy response.

> "Then the one who had received the one talent also came forward, saying, 'Master, I knew that you were a harsh man, reaping where you did not sow, and gathering where you did not scatter seed; so I was afraid, and I went and hid your talent in the ground.'" (Matthew 25:24-25)

The cycle is this: Ignorance (*"I knew that you were a harsh man"*) begets fear (*"so I was afraid"*), which leads to idleness (*"I went and hid your talent in the ground"*).

The third servant was mired in fear because he never bothered getting to know the Master. Had he made any effort whatsoever, he would have realized that the desire of the Master was not to punish, but to reward His servants:

> "You knew, did you, that I reap where I did not sow, and gather where I did not scatter? Then you ought to have invested my money with the bankers, and on my return I would have received what was my own with interest."
> (Matthew 25:26-27)

Are you picking up the Master's angst here? All he asked of the servant was to do *something* with what He was entrusted with. Instead he did nothing. Waiting for someday to do something is a dangerous game.

There are too many churches that bury their talents, their provision from God, in the ground. And there are too many churches that are controlled by fear, more concerned about "meeting budget" than making disciples. Frankly, it raises the question of whether churches that are mired in fear actually know God. This is admittedly harsh, but not unreasonably so, for if we truly grasp who God is we would be quick to step out in faith rather than remain stuck in fear.

In contrast to the third servant, the first and second servants did in fact know the Master, and responded to Him in a "good and faithful" manner.

But we shouldn't assume it was easy for them to reach that point. In fact, it's reasonable to wonder if these two servants, like the third servant, may have been fearful of the Master at some point. Fear, after all, is a natural human emotion. But if the latter

195

two servants were fearful at one time, they didn't stay there. Instead, they studied the Master, communed with the Master, placed their faith in the Master, and stepped out in faith for the Master. They didn't wait for someday to do something. Rather, because they knew the Master, they acted "at once" (vs. 16).

Church leaders who stay connected with the Master are positioned to respond to the Master in faith. The pressures of ministry, financial and otherwise, don't hold sway over them because in increasingly knowing the Master they increasingly trust the Master.

The parable closes with a reminder that God rewards those who act in accordance with their faith:

"I will put you in charge of many things; enter into the joy of your master."(Matthew 25:21, 23)

FAITH-BASED BUDGETING

Establishing a church budget is one of the most difficult tasks church leaders face. But I believe that some leaders make it much harder on themselves than it ought to be. The difficult task of budgeting is made much worse when leaders value financial stability over spiritual vitality, financial management over biblical stewardship, and preservation over supplication. Each of these, you will notice, are ongoing rather than time-bound considerations. What we value and focus on throughout the year informs how we go about discerning a budget in season.

Many churches make the mistake of assessing their health through a strictly quantitative lens. For them, attendance and giving levels take precedence over making disciples and loving God and neighbor. Quantitative metrics are important to be sure, but strong numeric performance does not necessarily equate to a healthy church. One of the most Spirit filled churches I have ever set foot in was a cramped, rustic, dirt floor church in Cap-Haïtien, Haiti. Cross to Light Church[28] doesn't have much in the way of finances or space, but they are very, very healthy – much more so than some large, wealthy churches that are spiritually bankrupt. Budgeting gets a whole lot easier when we put first things first.

Budgeting also gets easier when we emphasize biblical stewardship over financial management. Don't get me wrong, churches *do* need to be adept at financial management, and are blessed when they have leaders who are highly skilled in this area. But of much greater importance is having a leadership team committed to preaching, teaching, and modeling biblical stewardship in its fullness, its vastness. Not everyone can be a sophisticated, shrewd manager of money. But everyone can be a good, faithful steward. Show me a church filled with good stewards, and I'll show you a church that isn't burdened by the budgeting process.

Finally, budgeting becomes much easier when church leaders shift from trying to preserve what is to asking God to provide for what is yet to come. Churches that value preservation are those that cling to the status quo, budgeting the same amounts for the same line items year over year. But churches that value supplication are those that are on their knees, asking God to provide for the mission, vision, and plans that He has set before the church. Budgeting is much easier when we loosen our grip on what is, and pray that God will provide for what is yet to come.

As you go about discerning a budget that aligns with and

supports how God has led you to this point, I encourage you to take into account the following principles and considerations:

Select a budgeting approach that works for your church.
Aubrey Malphurs and Steve Stroope, in *Money Matters in Church: A Practical Guide for Leaders,* detail the two most common approaches for budgeting: the fundamentals approach, and the functions approach.[29] The fundamentals approach allocates funds to four fundamental areas, which are missions, personnel, programming, and facilities. The authors provide a guideline of 10% to missions, 50% to personnel, 20% to facilities, and 20% to programming. The second option is the functions approach, in which the budget is distributed to the church's main ministry functions, or purposes. Here, personnel expenses are tucked underneath a given function. I have used both approaches, and believe that both are viable. Choose the approach that works best for your church.

Consider providing a preliminary budget parameter.
While the budget must align with and support annual objectives, strategies, and ministry/department plans, it is helpful to have a preliminary idea of what the leadership believes the church can support in the coming fiscal year. However, the balance here is delicate – a preliminary budget parameter should not restrict leaders from dreaming and thinking big. Rather, it should help leaders to proactively think through what they can do now, and what may need to wait for later.

Set a budget that enables rather than restricts ministry.

Your budget ought to help ministries flourish rather than merely stay in place. But I have seen enough church budgets to realize that some view the budget not as a means of enabling ministry, but of controlling ministry. On the same hand, ministry and department leaders need to see the bigger picture, understanding that while their needs are important, so too are the needs of other ministries and departments. However you get there, strive to set a budget that enables key ministry priorities and moves the church as a whole forward.

Be intentional to create a faith-based budget.

Most churches release a budget that they believe will safely be met. But isn't this approach rooted more in fact (what we can see) than faith (what we can't see)? A faith-based budget adds a measure of faith to what we can see or project. For example, if the "safe" annual giving level of a church is believed to be $200,000, adding 5% as a measure of faith boosts the budget to $210,000.

Create a contingency plan to accompany the budget.

In tandem with the budget, churches are wise to release a contingency plan that describes how the church will steward their finances if actual giving levels are either significantly above or below budgeted giving levels. In the former case, if the Holy Spirit has inspired you to identify long-range plans, objectives, or strategies that require finances beyond what has been budgeted, let congregants know that if giving exceeds the budget, the church will be poised and ready to pursue the plans that God has set before them. In the latter case, identify in advance specific areas where expenses could either be delayed or stopped altogether. In both scenarios, a well discerned contingency plan allows the church to stay the course on its most critical priorities while avoiding pressurized, time sensitive decisions on important matters.

Establish and maintain reserve funds.
In most churches, giving fluctuates seasonally and as people join, leave, or experience significant life changes. Reserve funds are vital for riding the normal waves of ministry, and being able to respond to unexpected needs or ministry opportunities. As a baseline, I recommend that churches set aside 10% of their annual budget as a cash reserve, an additional 10% as a buildings and grounds reserve, and 5% as a Holy Spirit Discernment reserve. The first two funds are "just in case" coverage should the church experience a sharp decline in giving, or an unexpected building expense. The third fund positions the church to cooperate with the leading of the Holy Spirit. If reserve funds are new for your church, don't let the challenge of building these funds exasperate you. Instead, chip away, setting aside 2-3% annually in each fund for as long as it takes.

Be clear on how the church handles designated gifts.
I met with a group of deacons recently who informed me that while giving to the general budget is down, total giving is as strong as ever. Their issue, and the issue for

many churches, is that congregants are allowed to designate their giving for a specific ministry or cause. If this is allowed at your church, I urge you to change your approach. The biblical instruction is for God's people to bring the whole tithe to the storehouse[30], and to trust that it will be used for good purpose. Special offerings and other giving opportunities have their place, but should be determined, or at least approved, in advance by the leaders of the church.

Preach, teach, and model biblical stewardship.
Stewardship is multi-dimensional and should be taught as such. But as it relates to financial stewardship, be sure to teach on why we are to give, how we are to give, and where we are to give. Many churches touch on the first two points but not the third, which is critical given the vast number of causes to give to nowadays. Scripture seems to indicate that giving to the local church should come before other causes. But we should not assume that our congregants know or agree with this premise – hence the need to clearly spell out where to give.

Actively communicate your needs.
Many pastors and leaders are reluctant to communicate the financial needs of their church. Their unease usually stems from not wanting visitors or members to believe that the church is only interested in their money. While understandable, their reluctance is not biblical. A church that takes its mission call seriously and seeks to discern and follow God's leading has every right – and responsibility –

to convey their needs, and to ask people to help meet them. Tellingly, the Apostle Paul had no trouble in this area whatsoever (1 Cor. 16:1, 2 Cor. 8:9).

Establish a Planned Giving Program.
Every church should have a Planned Giving program in place, and should actively (yet gently) encourage members to include the church as a beneficiary on living trusts and wills. Think of it this way: If a person gives generously to the church during his or her life, isn't it reasonable to assume they would desire to do the same upon entering our Lord's nearer presence? Most people who tithe to their church in life are blessed to designate a tithe of their estate to the church upon their death. These legacy gifts are vital for helping churches pursue key initiatives and plans.

Make prayer, thanksgiving, and celebration a priority.
I don't believe that we can ever "over spiritualize" financial matters in the church. The National Football League may penalize its players for excessive celebrations, but the Church of Jesus Christ has no such restrictions. Faith-based churches are quick to recognize and give thanks to God for His provision.

ANNUAL MINISTRY PLAN

With leadership clarity and commitment to the mission and vision, and with annual objectives and strategies finalized and supported by ministry/department plans and a faith-based budget, now is the time to share your work.

The Annual Ministry Plan is a key tool for sharing how God has led the church, and inspiring members and visitors to get on board. And while the Ministry Plan is chock full of details and information, because of the good work you have done to this point, its content is largely already completed!

The Ministry Plan template provided as a key tool will walk you through how to lay out the plan, and what to include. When the plan is complete, write a cover letter to go with it and get it in the hands of congregants and regular attenders as soon as possible (at least two weeks prior to the annual congregational meeting, if your church goes that route). Be sure to produce extra copies for future visitors and members.

Because the Annual Ministry Plan is such an important document, you should consider hiring a graphic artist to create or finalize the document. Whether you create the plan in house or through an outside firm, be sure that your Annual Ministry Plan is inspiring and of high quality, reflecting the significance of its contents.

QUESTIONS FOR DISCUSSION & REFLECTION

- What does your current budget reveal about your church? What changes might you make in the budget to improve the heart condition of your church?

- How does "knowing" the Master impact our stewardship over what the Master entrusts to us?

- What "measure of faith" does your church take when setting a budget?

19

CAPITAL CAMPAIGN CONSIDERATIONS

Capital campaigns become necessary when a church's vision far exceeds its present reality. When done well, a capital campaign can produce marked spiritual growth, deeper unity in the body, widespread sacrificial giving, and stronger faith.

The purpose of this brief chapter is not to spell out how to go about planning and conducting a capital campaign, but to challenge you to think about whether a campaign is right for your church at this time, or in the near future. The good news is that if your church does decide to begin a campaign, there are many incredible resources to guide you down the path. Still, my recommendation is to hire a reputable capital campaign consultant to help direct the process and maximize the effectiveness of the campaign.

IT'S ALL ABOUT VISION

A clear, compelling vision is what drives a successful capital campaign. A Holy Spirit discerned vision communicated with enthusiasm, clarity, and regularity can turn the driest of bones into flesh. But a vague, uninspiring vision can turn healthy flesh into dry bones.

Is your vision clear and compelling? Before considering a capital campaign, take time to grapple with this question. Your vision should inspire and speak to the hearts and minds of congregants. You should feel confident that if you surveyed your members, they would speak about the vision with clarity and passion.

In addition to being clear and compelling, the vision must be big - God-sized. At any point in time, the vision of a church ought to be so large as to be seemingly unattainable – yet so inspiring that the vision is worth striving and sacrificing for. Jesus' Sermon on the Mount represented a clear, compelling vision of kingdom living. Yet taking hold of what Jesus conveyed is virtually impossible for us in the "already but not yet" time in which we live. The vision is just too big. Still, empowered by the Spirit who lives in us, we strive to take hold of what Christ has set before us, understanding that the journey is of much greater significance than the destination. This same "journey over destination" dynamic takes place in well discerned capital campaigns. The vision is unattainable *on our own strength*, yet worth striving and sacrificing for.

Capital campaigns typically follow a specific, rather than directional, vision. It's difficult to convince congregants that a new youth ministry center is necessary if there isn't a specific vision that the project points toward. However, if your vision is directional, don't be quick to discount a capital campaign. Instead, take time to consider where you are at in your understanding of the vision, whether you are ready to specify what to include in a capital campaign, and how it will help bring forth the vision.

ASSESSING READINESS

Beyond the vision, you must also grapple with whether or not your church is ready for a capital campaign. Capital campaigns require an extremely high level of commitment from pastors, leaders, staff, and congregations. Capital campaigns can be invigorating, but also very, very exhausting, especially for those directly involved.

For this reason, it is a good idea for pastors to honestly and prayerfully consider their call to serving the church for at least the next three years. A pastor, especially a lead pastor, who senses imminent closure to his or her current ministry is cause enough to press the pause button before proceeding with a capital campaign. The staff and leadership must also honestly consider their commitment to a capital campaign. To proceed, key leaders must be on board, ready to both lead and participate.

Church leaders should also consider whether a capital campaign will help bring about mission attainment, or create mission distraction. If a campaign aligns clearly with the vision, and the vision clearly supports the mission, the church should be fine. But leaders must recognize that because capital campaigns can be very consuming, there is risk of the campaign overshadowing the mission. This is why leaders must be steadfast to hold on to the mission above all else.

PART SIX

EXECUTION

*"However beautiful the strategy, you should
occasionally look at the results."*
Sir Winston Churchill

Of the six steps in Faith-Based, two are by far the most likely to be overlooked: Preparation and Execution. Preparation gets overlooked by leaders who want to roll up their sleeves and get to work rather than getting on their knees and praying. Execution gets overlooked by leaders who are energized and focused when formulating plans, but lethargic and distracted when it comes to the much harder work of implementing plans. Interestingly, but not coincidentally, I have found that when teams don't prepare well going into a planning season, they don't execute well coming out of a planning season. All six steps work together, and all are challenging. But execution is especially challenging, mostly because whereas the first five steps typically take around a month each to complete, execution can stretch throughout the entire fiscal year.

As planning segues into execution, it is important to avoid the mistake of doing too much too soon, which brings frustration and fatigue. Execution is most effective not as a sprint but as a marathon, where diligence, adaptability, and persistence bring steady, sustainable forward movement.

Running a good race is commendable, but winning the race is what we're really after. And to win the race, we must, at all times and in all circumstances, follow where the Holy Spirit leads. Just as we have followed the Holy Spirit to discern our plans, so must we follow the Holy Spirit when implementing plans. Don't be surprised if the Spirit redirects your plans … and don't hesitate to depart from one plan in order to step into another.

20

EIGHT LESSONS IN EXECUTION

A cts 2 provides a vivid picture of the intersection between faith-based leadership and the work of the Holy Spirit. This combination gave birth to the early church, and has fueled thriving churches ever since.

Lesson 1: The Holy Spirit shows up when leaders are united in Christ and focused on God.

> "When the day of Pentecost came, they were all together in one place." (Acts 2:1)

The believers were together because Jesus had instructed them to stay in Jerusalem and wait for the baptism of the Holy Spirit (Acts 1:4-5). They willingly followed Jesus' instructions, fixing their focus on God as they joined together "constantly in prayer" (Acts 1:14).

Like the early leaders in Christ's church, your leadership team must gather regularly to worship, pray, and wait on the Holy Spirit. Doing so fosters trust, courage, and purpose.

Could the early church have formed without the Holy Spirit's involvement? Not hardly. It was the Holy Spirit who galvanized the believers, moving them from fear to faith. But what about us? If we go it alone, giving lip service to seeking and following the Holy Spirit but turning to ourselves when things don't go as planned, we lack faith and cannot expect the Spirit to work in our midst. Just as the early church drew its life from the Holy Spirit, so must we.

Lesson 2: When and how the Holy Spirit works is not for us to know.

> "Suddenly a sound like the blowing of a violent wind came from heaven and filled the whole house where they were sitting. They saw what seemed to be tongues of fire that separated and came to rest on each of them." (Acts 2:2-3)

Jesus told His followers to gather in Jerusalem to receive the baptism of the Holy Spirit. But Jesus did not tell them when or how this would happen.

Our natural bent is to want immediate answers to our questions, immediate solutions to our problems, and immediate clarity for our future. But if we had all of that, would we need faith?

Make no mistake, there will be times when implementing your plans will seem impossible. The opposition will seem too fierce, the energy required too high, the budget too low. But faith-based leaders embrace uncertainty, knowing that it is during uncertain times that our faith is made strong. And faith-based leaders remain both persistent and patient – persistent to seek the Holy Spirit, and patient to wait on the Holy Spirit.

Faith-based leaders also understand that how the Holy Spirit works is not ours to determine. Yes, the Holy Spirit can work dramatically and unmistakably as with those gathered in Jerusalem, but most often the Spirit speaks to us much more subtly. I can't begin to count the times when something that had me perplexed became suddenly very clear after reading scripture, or conversing with a brother or sister, or praying, or worshipping. Coincidence? Not at all. This is the work of the Holy Spirit.

Lesson 3: The Holy Spirit brings unity through diversity.

> "All of them were filled with the Holy Spirit and began to speak in other tongues as the Spirit enabled them."
> (Acts 2:4)

Nearly 4,000 years before enabling the crowd gathered in Jerusalem to speak other languages, the Holy Spirit did the same thing with a group gathered in Shinar. But unlike those gathered in Jerusalem, the people in Shinar weren't seeking God, they were rebelling against God. Still, while the circumstances could not have been more different, in both cases the Holy Spirit enabled the people to speak a variety of languages so that God's people could step into God's plan. In Shinar, the new languages confused the people, prompting them to drop their tower project in favor of scattering the earth and increasing in number - just as God had previously commanded them. In Jerusalem, where at least fifteen different people groups gathered,[31] the new languages brought not confusion but clarity, not division but unity.

As your leadership team works to execute the plans God has set before you, there will be a variety of thoughts and ideas for how to go about doing so. At times, there may be such breadth of opinions that it will seem as if your leaders aren't even speaking the same language! But if your leaders truly seek to be led by the Holy Spirit, then by the power of the Holy Spirit your team will experience deep, abiding unity in Christ, and one another. Left to ourselves, our diversity – of thought, background, ethnicity, gender – will divide us. But when we are fully surrendered to the Holy Spirit, our diversity is beautiful to behold, strengthening and uniting our leaders, and our church.

Lesson 4: Collaboration is key for discerning and following the leading of the Holy Spirit.

> "Amazed and perplexed, they asked one another, 'What does this mean?'" (Acts 2:12)

The manifestation of the Holy Spirit was so powerful that the people were "amazed," yet so unpredictable that they were "perplexed." Thus, the people wisely asked one another what all of this meant, and received their answer in short order from Peter (see lesson 6).

When we sense the Holy Spirit working in our midst, yet are unsure about what the Spirit is conveying specifically or how we are to respond, we need to ask one another, "What does this mean?" Collaboration is vital for understanding and following the leading of the Holy Spirit, and when we fail to consult with one another, we risk missing out on all that the Holy Spirit is inviting us into.

But collaboration with one another is incomplete. We must also collaborate with the Holy Spirit, understanding that the Holy Spirit is not out to confuse or frustrate us, but to guide us into truth (John 16:13), and to give us peace (1 Cor. 14:33).

Perhaps the most powerful, effective way of seeking answers to the "what does it mean" question is for a group of leaders to turn as one to scripture, asking the Holy Spirit to speak through the unchanging truth of God's Word. And as leaders listen for the Holy Spirit to speak through scripture, they must also listen for the Holy Spirit to speak through one another:

> "Without counsel plans fail, but with many advisers they succeed" (Proverbs 15:22).

Lesson 5: When following the Holy Spirit, expect ridicule and opposition.

> "Some, however, made fun of them and said, 'They have had too much wine.'" (Acts 2:13)

The more that leaders step into the call of Christ and follow the leading of the Holy Spirit, the more that leaders can expect ridicule and opposition – if not from within the church, most certainly from outside of the church.

A few days ago I met with a pastor who is leading his church to shift its focus from taking care of themselves to making disciples. This pastor is not pursuing some radical agenda, he's simply seeking to carry out the Great Commission (which admittedly is radical in itself). As we spoke, he told me about some letters he recently received from a few upset congregants. When I pressed him on what they were complaining about, two things jumped out at me: First, that their complaints were based entirely on personal preference rather than biblical truth, and second, that their complaints were overtly personal, intended to degrade the pastor.

On another occasion, I met with a pastor who had recently planted a church that quickly flourished, bringing many people to salvation in Jesus Christ. The leaders and members of this church were united, yet faced passive-aggressive opposition from outside their church – from some in the community, from some in their parent church, from some in the church they rented space from, even from some in their own denomination. This church dared to be different, dared to follow the leading of the Holy Spirit all the way, and for that they faced a good deal of opposition.

The good news is that while facing ridicule and opposition doesn't feel good, if it comes out of following the leading of the Holy Spirit, it *is* good.

Lesson 6: Above all else, proclaim the Gospel!

"Then Peter stood up with the Eleven, raised his voice and addressed the crowd: 'Fellow Jews and all of you who live in Jerusalem, let me explain this to you; listen carefully to what I say.'" (Acts 2:14)

It is possible to be so focused on implementing new and exciting initiatives that we lose sight of our primary call to proclaim the Gospel. Paul instructed his protégé Timothy to, "proclaim the message; be persistent whether the time is favorable or unfavorable."[32] Like Timothy, we too must be steadfast in proclaiming the Gospel at all times.

Imagine if in Jerusalem the people asking, "what does this mean," received no response. Or worse that Peter, himself amazed and perplexed at the wondrous working of the Holy Spirit, answered their question with, "Fellow Jews and all of you who live in Jerusalem, we don't know what this means! We were just told to stay here and receive the Holy Spirit, and then all of this happened. But rest assured that we will be forming a committee to discuss what this means, and once we figure it out, we'll call a meeting to let you know."

Thankfully, that didn't happen! Instead, Peter answered their question by proclaiming the Gospel. He began with a prophecy from Joel to remind the people of God's promises, then connected the prophecy to the life, death, and resurrection of Jesus Christ.

As you implement objectives and strategies, there will be some who ask, "What does this mean?" Rather than becoming frustrated by their inability to "get" it, consider their questions a gift, offering fresh opportunities to connect your plans to the Gospel, and to share how your plans will help make disciples. And above all else, continue to proclaim the Gospel, in season and out of season, in times both favorable and unfavorable.

Lesson 7: Be ready to reap the harvest.

> "When the people heard this, they were cut to the heart and
> said to Peter and the other apostles, 'Brothers, what shall
> we do?' Peter replied, 'Repent and be baptized, every one
> of you, in the name of Jesus Christ for the forgiveness of
> your sins. And you will receive the gift of the Holy Spirit.'"
> (Acts 2:37-38)

When people believe the Gospel message of salvation in Christ for
the very first time, they naturally ask, "What shall I do?"
Sometimes the question is asked aloud, other times in silence. In
the former case, the answer we ought to give is essentially the
answer Peter gave to those gathered in Jerusalem: Repent and
receive Jesus Christ as your Savior and Lord. But the latter case is
much more challenging because to "hear" a person asking an
unspoken question requires strong spiritual acuity, which not
everyone possesses. For this reason, the best approach toward
those who hear the Gospel but don't verbally ask how to respond
is to simply ask them if they are ready to place their faith in Jesus
Christ. When the seeds of the Gospel have been sown, we need to
be ready and willing to reap the harvest.

I realize that what I am describing here is Evangelism 101, but
it merits a mention because in truth many church members are not
inclined to share the Gospel, or to invite a person to take a step of
faith, or even to invite a person to a worship service.

LifeWay Research conducted a recent study of churchgoing
American Protestants that revealed that 80 percent of those who
attend church one or more times a month believe they have a

personal responsibility to share their faith, yet only 39 percent have told another person about how to become a Christian in the previous six months.[33] And Dr. Thom Rainer, in *The Unchurched Next Door*, reports that only two percent of church members invite an unchurched person to church in a given year.[34]

The workers may be few, but there is no excuse to not reap the harvest *in our own backyard*. Let us never be so sidetracked by implementing plans that we fail to proclaim the Gospel, and to invite those who hear the Gospel to place their faith in Jesus Christ.

Lesson 8: Trust God to bring the increase.

> "Those who accepted his message were baptized, and about three thousand were added to their number that day." (Acts 2:41)

When you read Acts 2:41, what immediately comes to mind? If you're like most people, it's the fact that three thousand people came to Christ in one fell swoop. Talk about a good day for evangelism! But while it's appropriate to celebrate this amazing response to the Gospel, if we're not careful we'll miss the rest of the story.

Let's go back a few verses. After Peter proclaims the Gospel, the people are cut to the heart and wonder how to respond to what they've just heard. Peter exhorts them to, "Repent and be baptized, *every one* of you." Peter's invitation excluded no one; it was for "every one." So while it's appropriate to rejoice over three thousand people coming to Christ that day, it's also appropriate to recognize that there were scores of people who *rejected* the Gospel message that same day.

How many? We don't know, but it's reasonable to surmise that those gathered in Jerusalem didn't number in the thousands, but in the hundreds of thousands. Suffice to say, there were many more who heard the Gospel and rejected it than those who heard the Gospel and accepted it.

For context, consider what the Jewish historian Josephus wrote about the Passover feast during the days of Nero:

> "And that this city could contain so many people in it is manifest by that number of them which was taken under Cestius, who being desirous of informing Nero of the power of the city, who otherwise was disposed to condemn that nation, entreated the high priests, if the thing were possible, to take the number of their whole multitude. So these high priests, upon the coming of their feast which is called the Passover, when they slay their sacrifices, from the ninth hour to the eleventh, but so that a company not less than ten belong to every sacrifice (for it is not lawful for them to feast singly by themselves), and many of us are twenty in a company, found the number of sacrifices was two hundred fifty-six thousand five hundred; which, upon the allowance of no more than ten that feast together, amounts to two million seven hundred thousand two hundred persons that were pure and holy."[35]

While Passover brought more people to Jerusalem than Pentecost, there is little question that massive crowds were gathered in Jerusalem on the Day of Pentecost, 33 A.D.

This represents a simple yet critically important reminder that God alone brings the increase. Peter proclaimed the Gospel passionately and persuasively, and while many placed their faith in Christ, many more did not. Yet even if one person would have accepted the Gospel message that day, the occasion would have been worth celebrating!

When it comes to salvation, the distinction between our role and God's role could not be more important to grasp. We are called to be faithful in proclaiming the Gospel, but we have no ability to bring salvation to a person – that is God's work alone. Yes, God allows us to partake in what He is doing, but only God can pardon people of their sin. All of this is vitally important for many reasons, not least of which is that if we don't accept this reality we will invariably either take credit we don't deserve when people accept the Gospel, or bear guilt we don't deserve when people don't. Our role is to be faithful in proclaiming and living in accordance with the Gospel, and to trust God to bring the increase.

QUESTIONS FOR DISCUSSION & REFLECTION

- When it comes to execution, is the pattern at your church to try to do too much too soon? Or to wait too long to get started? Or does your leadership do well at holding a steady pace that brings sustainable forward movement?

- In looking at Acts 2, is there a particular lesson that your leadership team tends to excel at? Why?

- Is there a lesson that your leadership struggles with? Are there changes that might help?

21

SPIRITUAL FARMING, PART TWO

In Assessment we examined several farming elements that are essential for growing disciples. We considered how both the climate of a church and the spiritual rootedness of leaders and congregants impact our pace of change. We thought about the soil of our church, and how best to work the soil to help bring growth. Finally, we considered our approach to seeding, and the need for grafting. We examined these elements in order to assess where we were as leaders and as a church, and to formulate plans that position us for growth in the coming season.

Having established our plans, it's time now to consider how three additional farming elements – light, water, and fertilizer - serve to bring our plans to fruition.

Just as sunlight is necessary for citrus trees to bear fruit, so too is *Son*light necessary for churches to bear fruit. But many churches, and many church leaders, choose instead to remain in shadows, where nothing can grow. Water too is requisite for growth, but both underwatering and overwatering can significantly diminish fruitfulness. And fertilizer helps spur growth, but if we're not careful, too much fertilizer can kill what we're trying to grow. Let us now consider how to best manage each of these elements.

LIGHT

> "Live as children of light (for the fruit of the light consists in all goodness, righteousness and truth) and find out what pleases the Lord. Have nothing to do with the fruitless deeds of darkness, but rather expose them." (Eph. 5:8-11)

Living in darkness produces no fruit, while living in the light of Christ brings an abundant harvest. Yet so many Christians, including pastors and leaders, remain in the dark, where nothing grows. Shadow dwellers are those who are unwilling to reveal their deepest, darkest struggles to God, or for that matter to other people. And when leaders hide in the shadows, whole churches suffer. As the leaders go, so goes the church.

Paul was not exhorting the Ephesian Christians to expose the fruitless deeds of darkness of other people; he was exhorting them to expose *their own* fruitless deeds of darkness. And while our natural bent is to point out other people's sin before exposing our own, living in the light requires that we flip the script. Ongoing exposure to light can be very uncomfortable, but ultimately living in light is what brings healing and wholeness, growth and fruit.

Imagine that a patient is preparing for a surgical procedure. Before the anesthesia is administered, the thought enters his mind that the surgeon, along with the other doctors and nurses involved, will see him completely exposed, under the brightest of lights. This makes him so uncomfortable that he asks for a private conversation with the surgeon, asking the surgeon to perform the surgery in the dark, which by his reckoning should be just fine since the surgeon would have done this procedure countless times before.

Can you imagine this scenario actually taking place? Not a chance! But it begs some hard questions: Why do we expect God to bring healing and wholeness to our lives, and to our churches, when we ourselves are unwilling to step into the light to fully expose our sin? Doesn't a personal relationship with Jesus Christ merit prayers that are heartfelt and personal? Shouldn't our call as church leaders compel us to set the example for others by stepping courageously into the light, rather than remaining anonymous in the shadows?

As followers of Jesus Christ, and as leaders in Christ's church, we must take up residency in the light of Christ. We must, like the Psalmist, invite God to search our hearts – at all times, and in all circumstances – and to lead us in the way everlasting. And we must selectively share our deepest struggles – not publicly, but with a trusted brother or sister who can provide wise counsel and earnest prayer. This is how iron sharpens iron. This is how we live in the light.

If you're confused as to why I've included living in light in a section on executing strategic plans, allow me to explain. I have been a part of numerous church leadership teams. Most have done well in stepping into and leading from light, but a few have not. Without exception, the teams that stepped into light were much more successful in implementing plans than those that remained in shadows. The teams that made prayer a priority rather than a formality harvested more fruit. The teams whose leaders were willing to confess and ask forgiveness for their personal sins, and for the corporate sins of the church, harvested more fruit. And like the four friends who lowered their paralyzed friend through a roof to see Jesus, the teams whose leaders were willing to carry others, and to allow others to carry them, harvested more fruit.

We can have the very best plans, with the very best intentions of executing our plans, but in the absence of light, we will not see fruit.

WATER

> "Too little water and the tree will die. Too much and the tree will die. This can leave even an experienced gardener asking 'How often do I water a citrus tree?'"
>
> *Tips on Water Requirements for Citrus Trees*, from gardeningknowhow.com

Just as an orange tree can't grow without water, neither can a church. Yet just as an orange tree can drown if it takes on too much water, so too can a church. A multi-faceted watering plan designed to sustain growth and reap a harvest is essential. The watering plan should address both long-term priorities (mission, vision, and values) and annual plans (objectives, strategies, ministry/department plans). The watering plan does not need to be complex, but it does need to be well thought out and diligently adhered to.

Watering long-term priorities

Your mission of making disciples of Jesus Christ must be conveyed regularly, in a variety of ways and in a variety of settings. The watering plan for the mission should entail how and when you will convey the mission – from the pulpit, in discipleship classes, new member orientation, brochures, etc. There is absolutely no risk of over watering mission, but there is a high risk of under watering mission. I have been in churches that treated their mission as an afterthought, which pretty well guarantees that it will never come to fruition. Conversely, I was in a church recently that featured its mission statement *everywhere*, even on a wall adjoining the worship center. Anyone who sets foot in this church knows what the church stands for. And not coincidentally, this church is a rapidly growing, healthy and vibrant church. To see your mission come to fruition, be sure to water the mission frequently, using a variety of approaches.

Whether specific or directional, the vision of your church must be cast repeatedly. It has been said that "vision leaks," and I for one couldn't agree more. That being the case, the best way to deal with water loss is to continually add fresh water. Vision, by definition, is a future state, and because people naturally fixate on what is in front of them, the need to convey what *could be*, rather than what is, cannot be overstated. Just as we cannot drown mission, neither can we drown vision. So keep watering!

Values also require much water, albeit less than mission and vision. A watering plan for values can entail highlighting a single core value on a cyclical basis. For example, if a church holds six core values, it could highlight a "value of the month" over a six-month period. Ultimately, the best way to ensure that stated values are actual values is for leaders to actively live out the values, and to encourage others to do so as well.

Watering annual plans

Unlike long-term priorities that require frequent watering, annual plans require a more nuanced watering plan.

Objectives and strategies should be communicated clearly to the congregation via the annual ministry plan, and from the pulpit at the onset of a new fiscal year. Additional communication should take place periodically throughout the year. In my experience, an effective watering plan for communicating objectives and strategies to the congregation is to publish a standard quarterly update, along with additional updates when there are significant developments. The intent is to remind congregants of key initiatives, and to rekindle enthusiasm. When it comes to watering annual plans, moderation is more effective than saturation.

However, for leaders, staff, and church members who are directly involved in implementing a given objective or strategy, planning meetings and status updates must be much more frequent – at least monthly and, depending on the nature of the objective or strategy, as much as weekly. Progress reports should be given at least monthly to staff and leadership, with an invitation to collaboratively troubleshoot issues and remove roadblocks.

As for ministry/department plans, a balanced watering plan includes updates to other staff members monthly, and to the broader leadership team quarterly. Additional updates should be given regularly to volunteers and participants in each ministry or department. Communication to the congregation relative to ministry/department plans should happen when there is a significant development that affects a large segment of the congregation. For example, a change in the literature placed at the guest services desk doesn't merit an update to the congregation, but a change to the children's Sunday school curriculum does.

Your plans are vitally important! Take time to develop and carry out a watering plan that helps your plans – and your church – grow and bear fruit.

FERTILIZER

"Fertilizer does no good in a heap, but a little spread around works miracles all over."

Richard Brinsley Sheridan

Light and water provide ongoing nourishment and steady growth. But there are times when growth must be accelerated in order for fruit to be more fully realized. This is where fertilizer comes into play.

Suppose a church identified an objective to, "Begin a ministry to help at-risk children at the local elementary school." Further suppose that this objective was supported by several strategies, including finding and partnering with a parachurch ministry that has demonstrated success with at-risk children, recruiting a stable of mentors, and asking the school how the church might be a blessing to them, and to the parents and families of at-risk children. In short order, Kids Hope USA[36] is selected as a partner organization, and the school is enthusiastic about how a local church can help their cause. But recruiting mentors is painfully slow, and there is concern that the new ministry may never get off the ground. After a recent status update to church leadership, the leaders and implementation team agree that it is time to add fertilizer.

A few weeks later, the principle of the elementary school comes to the church and is given three minutes to speak to the congregation. Speaking from the heart and with conviction, the principle conveys the need for at risk children to be mentored, and for essential items such as backpacks and school supplies to be provided for some of their students. The principle closes by expressing appreciation to the church for getting involved. Afterwards, the pastor appeals to the congregation to prayerfully consider being a mentor, and to donate toward backpacks and school supplies. The pastor closes by giving clear instructions for how members can sign up to mentor, and provide supplies. The Holy Spirit does the rest as a dozen people sign up over the next two weeks to mentor, and school supplies are collected and given to the school. The fertilizer applied to the objective has made all the difference; a new ministry has been born!

The example is not at all far-fetched. In fact, both of the churches I have served have a Kids Hope USA ministry, and one of them had launched the ministry right before I came on board. The ministry director told me that when they were preparing to launch, there were initially very few mentors – barely enough to start - until the lead pastor made a personal appeal on a Sunday morning. Later, when still more mentors were needed, the school principle spoke, and more people stepped forward. Today, this church has a thriving mentoring ministry and a deep partnership with the school that has helped transform kids and families.

The likelihood is high that you will need to add fertilizer at least once to every objective and strategy. Fertilizer is a powerful tool for accelerating growth and bringing increased fruition. But care should be taken to avoid over fertilizing. Once a good dose of fertilizer is applied, provide space for the Holy Spirit to work. If you find yourself applying fertilizer time and time again, chances are you're desperately trying to make something work that just isn't there. Instead, take a break to pray and discern how (or whether) to go forward with the objective or strategy.

QUESTIONS FOR DISCUSSION & REFLECTION

- Why is living in, and leading from, light so vital for executing plans?

- Why do long-range priorities (mission, vision, values) require so much more water than annual plans (objectives, strategies, ministry/department plans)?

- How might fertilizer help bring plans to fruition?

22

FAITH-BASED DECISION MAKING

Even as you diligently and persistently set out to execute plans, it is inevitable that your leadership team will encounter a variety of unforeseen challenges and unplanned opportunities. The decision making model that follows is tried and tested, and will assist your leadership team to make God honoring, Spirit led decisions. If the model looks familiar, that's because it is! It's the same as the 5x5 Annual Planning model, albeit with a different application.

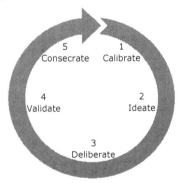

Before beginning a decision making process, take a moment to verify that the issue at hand is legitimate. Your time and focus is valuable, and should not be wasted chasing after phantom problems. If you're going to invest in decision making, invest beforehand in making sure that the issue being presented is a legitimate issue that merits leadership focus and attention.

The decision making process begins by calibrating ourselves to God. Just about every pastor and church leader can think of times when key decisions were made without stopping to pray, or to seek the leading of the Holy Spirit – times when we trusted ourselves more than God. *Calibration* requires intentionality and comes through prayer, an express desire to glorify God, inviting the Holy Spirit to guide and direct us, and a commitment to act in faith rather than fear or fact.

Ideation is when we form ideas and solutions. This step is straightforward but often overlooked. Many leadership teams gravitate to convenient solutions, rather than allowing time and space for creative, out of the box ideas to emerge. Can you think of a time when your leadership team latched on to the first good idea and regretted it later? Most of us have had that experience, perhaps more often than we care to admit!

To *deliberate* is to think about or discuss something very carefully in order to make a decision. As leaders work through proposed ideas and solutions, it is vital to seek the leading of the Holy Spirit, listen to the counsel of one another (Proverbs 11:14), count the cost of various options, and take into account the opportunities that the issue or challenge provides (Eph. 5:15-16).

When the time comes to *validate* our decision, we do so by verifying one last time that what we have decided does not go against the grain of scripture in any way, and aligns with and supports our mission, vision, values, and annual plans.

Finally, when we have made a decision, we *consecrate* it to the Lord. Part of consecration is simply calling for the question, reminding leaders to, "Let what you say be simply 'Yes' or 'No'" (Matthew 5:37). When the decision is finalized, leaders must be united in their support of it and of one another (Ephesians 4:3). And leaders must surrender their decision to God, inviting the Lord to do what only He can (Proverbs 16:3).

FAITH-BASED DECISION MAKING IN ACTION: THE CHOOSING OF THE SEVEN

Acts 6:1-7 represents an incredibly significant event in the formation of the early church. What took place propelled the church into a marked season of growth, while at the same time defining the role of a deacon. The leaders in the Jerusalem church have given us a wonderful example of faith-based decision making at its best.

As we examine what took place through the lens of the decision-making model, allow me to point out the obvious: Nowhere in Acts 6 do we find the words calibrate, ideate, deliberate, validate, or consecrate. But when we consider what the apostles decided, and how they made their decision, there is little question that their approach aligns with the model.

The Problem

> "In those days when the number of disciples was increasing, the Hellenistic Jews among them complained against the Hebraic Jews because their widows were being overlooked in the daily distribution of food." (Acts 6:1)

Before embarking on a decision-making process, we must first establish that the supposed problem is, in fact, a problem. In Jerusalem, the problem was clearly legitimate. Until recently these widows would have been taken care of through the weekly dole (Quppah), when baskets of food were given to the needy. But after they converted to Christianity, the responsibility for providing food moved from the temple to the church. The supposed problem was an actual problem that merited the attention of the apostles.

Calibration

> "So the Twelve gathered all the disciples together and said, 'It would not be right for us to neglect the ministry of the word of God in order to wait on tables.'" (Acts 6:2)

Before they gathered the other disciples, we can safely assume that the twelve took time to meet together, praying and seeking the leading of the Holy Spirit. With proper calibration, they were able to address the issue while safeguarding their primary ministry call to pray and preach the Gospel. Do you suppose it would have been tempting for the twelve to redirect their focus, even temporarily, to providing for the widows of the church? Given the sensitivity and potential divisiveness of the situation, that is a very real possibility. Thankfully, they took time to calibrate their hearts and minds to God, which gave them spiritual acuity.

Ideation, Deliberation, Validation

> "Brothers and sisters, choose seven men from among you who are known to be full of the Spirit and wisdom. We will turn this responsibility over to them and will give our

attention to prayer and the ministry of the word."
(Acts 6:3-4)

While the twelve very likely did not employ a linear process, somehow, someway they were able to advance a specific solution. And they could not have arrived there without some sort of ideation in which they bantered possible solutions, deliberation where they considered possible solutions in depth, and validation to make sure that their proposed solution supported rather than undermined their mission. Did they get it right?

> "This proposal pleased the whole group. They chose Stephen, a man full of faith and of the Holy Spirit; also Philip, Procorus, Nicanor, Timon, Parmenas, and Nicolas from Antioch, a convert to Judaism." (Acts 6:5)

"This proposal pleased the whole group" - how often does that happen at your church?! The apostles turned the decision over to the church, in essence beginning a new decision making process. The church got it right too. All of the names listed are Greek; all were Hellenistic Jews. It was the Hellenistic Jews who raised the complaint in the first place, so it's only fitting they be involved in the solution. But do you suppose it would have required significant trust on the part of the Hebraic Jews for this sort of solution to be put in place? Both parties are to be commended – the Hellenistic Jews for raising an issue and agreeing to take part in solving it, and the Hebraic Jews for trusting the Hellenistic Jews to act with wisdom and courage. This was one of the church's finest hours. But there was, of course, one more step …

Consecration

"They presented these men to the apostles, who prayed and laid their hands on them." (Acts 6:6)

All of them – the "whole group" (verse 6) - consecrated their decision to God, as the apostles prayed and laid hands on those who were selected. This is what a faith-based, consecrated decision looks like!

The Result

"So the word of God spread. The number of disciples in Jerusalem increased rapidly, and a large number of priests became obedient to the faith." (Acts 6:7)

Verse 1 stated that, "in those days the number of disciples was increasing." This tells us that prior to the naming of the seven the church was already growing. But adding the word "rapidly" in verse 7 brings a whole new dimension to what was happening in the church. The Greek word for rapidly is "sphodra,"[37] which can be translated to mean "exceedingly." The church had been growing steadily, but after the naming of the seven the church grew rapidly – *exceedingly*.

And we should not overlook the significance that among those who made up this rapid growth were, "a large number of priests." This is especially important because the opposition the church was facing in those days came primarily from Jewish priests. Thus, when many of these priests became open to the Gospel - "obedient to the faith" – it became clear that the truth of the

Gospel, and the forward movement of the church, would not be denied.

Faith-based decision making helped move the early church from looming division to rapid multiplication.

QUESTIONS FOR DISCUSSION & REFLECTION

- Have there been times in your leadership when prayer became an afterthought while dealing with a difficult issue?

- Do the leaders at your church allow ample time and space for creative ideas to emerge, or is the tendency to select practical ideas that surface quickly?

- What difficult challenges is your church facing today? How might the Decision Making model help guide your team to a well discerned, Holy Spirit inspired solution?

KEY TOOLS

KEY TOOL:

F.A.I.T.H. Filter

The *F.A.I.T.H. Filter* encapsulates five critical aspects that our plans must successfully pass through prior to being finalized. The filter helps to ensure that our plans are ...

Flexible ... held loosely; able to change as the Holy Spirit leads us.

Aligned ... with the Great Commission, and with our mission, vision and values.

Intertwined ... synergized and cohesive so that all of our plans represent a plan.

Transformational ... so that lives are changed by the grace and truth of Jesus Christ.

Holy ... set apart to God, consecrated to God ... fully surrendered to God.

Allow me to elaborate a bit on each of the five aspects:

Our plans need to be *Flexible* - held loosely. Why? Because we need to allow space for God to change our plans, and to accept that even if our plans are on the mark, God's timing likely won't match ours.

And our plans need to be *Aligned* - with Scripture, with the Great Commission, and with our mission, vision, and values. But more than that, as we look up and down the planning model, we need to make sure that all of the planning elements are properly aligned.

Our plans need to be *Intertwined* - synergized and cohesive to the point where our plans become a plan – a single plan, one that is comprehensive, cohesive, and church-wide.

Our plans need to be *Transformational* – they need to help bring people to Christ, and grow people in Christ. Our plans should be substantial enough to bring transformation to our church, community, and beyond, because good plans always facilitate movement, moving us from "here to there."

Finally, our plans must be *Holy* – set apart to God. Granted, unlike scripture our plans aren't "God-breathed," but they should be divinely inspired, prayed up, and fully surrendered to God.

I have found the *F.A.I.T.H. Filter* to be most effective when used at three different points in the planning process:

At the onset.
As you roll out the annual planning process, let your consistory and staff know that before anything is finalized, all plans will need to successfully pass through the

F.A.I.T.H. Filter. This helps leaders to immediately orient their thinking toward the five aspects of the filter.

When formulating plans.

I suppose this is self-evident, but oftentimes when clarity begins to emerge and plans are solidified, the *F.A.I.T.H. Filter* gets overlooked. Hopefully, the five aspects of the filter are already ingrained, but given our human tendency to wander, it's far from a sure thing. I recommend keeping the filter at the forefront when formulating plans.

When finalizing plans.

It is important that we run all of what we have done – objectives, strategies, ministry/department plans, staffing plan, budget, etc. – one last time through the *F.A.I.T.H. Filter* before finalizing and releasing our work. If nothing else, you'll be blessed by seeing how everything works together and points clearly to mission attainment. But don't be surprised if the need for a change - usually minor - emerges. Either way, applying the filter at this stage essentially stamps your plans as ready to release, believing in faith that God will bless your work to accomplish His purposes.

SAMPLE APPROACH FOR USING THE F.A.I.T.H. FILTER

Take your leaders through the following exercise as you begin your planning season:

Flexible: Read Acts 16:6-10. Are we willing and able to hold our plans loosely, adapting as necessary to the leading of the Holy Spirit?

Aligned: Read Matthew 28:18-20 and Matthew 22:37-39. Can we agree to make sure that our budget, HR plan, ministry/department plans, strategies, and objectives align with and support one another, in order to help bring about the mission and vision?

Intertwined: Read Acts 2:42-47. Can we agree to make sure that our plans hang together as a single, unified plan that reflects the purposes of the church?

Transformational: Read Romans 12:2 and 2 Corinthians 5:17. Will we work to ensure that our plans will help transform people? Our church? Community?

Holy: Read Colossians 1:18 and Proverbs 16:3. Let us pray as we joyfully and expectantly surrender our plans to God.

KEY TOOL:
Spiritual Farming Template

Just as producing an abundant harvest is the goal of conventional farming, so too is it the goal of spiritual farming. The template that follows is designed to help assess the climate, roots, soil, and seed of your church, so that in understanding where you are at presently, you are able to think clearly about where to go, and how to get there, in the future.

SPIRITUAL FARMING TEMPLATE

In general, what is the church climate at this time?	___ **Scorching Hot** (The heat is scorching; we are constantly under duress) ___ **Hot** (We feel the heat, but it's not typically scorching) ___ **Moderate** (We rarely face high heat; typically our climate is pleasant) ___ **Cold** (We hardly ever face high heat, but feel that perhaps we should)
How deep are the roots of your church at this time?	___ **Very Deep** (Able to grow and flourish in high heat) ___ **Deep** (Able to withstand, but not grow or flourish, in high heat) ___ **Moderate** (Able to withstand *some* heat, but not sustained high heat) ___ **Shallow** (Unable to withstand high heat; likely to wither)
What pace of change might be best for you in the forthcoming season?	___ **Rapid** (Our roots are very deep or deep in all three key areas - leadership, staff, and congregation) ___ **Steady** (Our roots are very deep, deep, or moderate in all three areas) ___ **Slow** (Our roots are very deep, deep, or moderate in at two key areas) ___ **Delay** (Our roots are shallow in at least two areas; our first priority is to work on deepening our roots)
What type of soil does the church have at this time? (Select all that apply)	___ **Hard** (We focus more on traditions, customs, and protocol than on making disciples) ___ **Rocky** (We place a higher value on conversion than on discipleship) ___ **Thorny** (We spend more time worrying, or discussing finances, or focusing on non-essentials, than on making disciples) ___ **Good** (Our soil is free of rocks and thorns, able to bring forth an abundant harvest)
List some preliminary ideas for how you might alter your soil going forward	
Which seeding approach does your church tend to lean toward?	___ **Single Seed** ___ **Grafting**

KEY TOOL:
Deep and Wide Exercise

"Therefore go and make disciples of all nations, baptizing them in the name of the Father and of the Son and of the Holy Spirit, and teaching them to obey everything I have commanded you. And surely I am with you always, to the very end of the age."
Matthew 28:19

The mission that Christ has placed on His people, and on His church, is both wide *("Go")* and deep *("make disciples")*. We are to bring people to Christ ("baptizing them"), and help people become like Christ ("teaching them"). In essence, to be deep and wide is to be fully committed to, and demonstrably effective in, both evangelism and discipleship.

This simple exercise can be done in very little time, but the results are unfailingly revealing and represent an important input into the planning process.

The approach is straightforward: as a leadership team, begin by discussing what it means to excel as a church in each dimension (deep and wide). Then, using the 1-10 scale shown on the grid that follows, invite each person to give a personal assessment of where they feel the church is at presently. I recommend that this part be done discretely, perhaps by using sticky notes, and then averaged to get an aggregate score. However, if the team is more comfortable doing the assessment as a whole team, by all means do so! Just be sure to invite everyone to participate.

When you are ready, plot the results on the grid that follows:

Here are some questions to discuss as a team:

> Does the assessment surprise you in any way?

> In what ways might the assessment results help to inform and shape your planning?

> Is it possible for a church to be well above or above average at being "Deep," yet well below or below average in being "Wide?" Why or why not?

> What would the impact be if you were able to raise the score for each dimension by one point in the next year?

KEY TOOL:
Leadership Covenant Example

I have found that having a well discerned, easy to understand Leadership Covenant is a great way to uphold core values and biblical truths in tandem with promoting cohesion and unity in Christ.

The Leadership Covenant example that follows is one I have used for several years. It was adapted from a similar covenant I had come across many years ago, but I have been unable to find the original source. The covenant encapsulates what we most ardently wish for our staff and leaders to commit to, understanding that if we are together on these things, the church as a whole will be more likely to follow suit.

The covenant is used in four ways: as a pre-employment requirement for staff members; a pre-nominations requirement for elders and deacons; an annual requirement for current staff members, elders, and deacons; and, on occasion, a tool for helping to resolve conflict.

There are two cautions that come with using a Leadership Covenant. The first is to avoid making the covenant legalistic, both in content and application. Don't include every minute theological position you hold, but rather list what you believe to be most essential for leaders to agree on. Then, after the covenant is signed, refrain from monitoring individual adherence to the covenant.

The covenant is meant to be entered into with good faith and best intentions, and pestering people about how they're doing with it will create an environment of legalism and mistrust. Once people sign it, trust that they'll own it for themselves.

The second caution is simply to recognize that while Leadership Covenants are helpful, they are not a cure all. If you have a staff or leadership team that is marked by dissension, lethargy, or conflict-avoidance, a Leadership Covenant will not in itself alter those behaviors. The covenant will help, but it cannot solve deeply rooted issues.

Nevertheless, I encourage you to develop a Leadership Covenant that lists what is most essential for leaders to agree on, and trust your leaders to make good on their commitment.

SAMPLE ANNUAL LEADERSHIP COVENANT

_____ I concur with the mission and core values that [Your Church] holds, and with God's help will endeavor to actively support and conduct myself in accordance with all.

_____ I have a personal relationship with Jesus Christ, as evidenced in my commitment to worship, Bible study, discipleship, fellowship and prayer.

> "Let us not give up meeting together... let us encourage one another." (Hebrews 10:25)

> "They devoted themselves to the Apostles' teaching and to fellowship, to the breaking of bread, and to prayer ... they continued to meet together in the temple courts. They broke bread together with glad and sincere hearts." (Acts 2:42, 46)

"Let the word of Christ dwell in you richly as you teach and admonish one another with all wisdom, and as you sing psalms, hymns and spiritual songs with gratitude in your hearts to God." (Colossians 3:16)

_____ **I am committed to the ministry of [Your Church], excited about the possibilities for ministry in our community and beyond, and supportive of the leadership of the church.**

"Then Jesus came to them and said, 'All authority in heaven and on earth has been given to me. Therefore, go and make disciples of all nations, baptizing them in the name of the Father and of the Son and of the Holy Spirit, and teaching them to obey everything I have commanded you. And surely I am with you always, to the very end of the age.'" (Matthew 28:16-20)

"You will receive power when the Holy Spirit comes on you; and you will be my witnesses in Jerusalem, and in all Judea and Samaria, and to the ends of the earth." (Acts 1:8)

"Give everyone what you owe him: if you owe taxes, pay taxes; if revenue, then revenue; if respect, then respect; if honor, then honor." (Romans 13:7)

_____ **I bring a teachable spirit into my position.**

"My sheep listen to my voice; I know them, and they follow me." (John 10:27)

"By grace you have been saved, through faith – and this is not from yourselves, it is the gift of God – not by works, so that no one can boast. For we are God's workmanship, created in Christ Jesus to do good works, which God prepared in advance for us to do." (Ephesians 2:8-10)

"You, however, are controlled not by the sinful nature but by the Spirit, if the Spirit of Christ lives in you. And if anyone does not have the Spirit of Christ, he does not belong to Christ." (Romans 8:9)

_____ I trust God and have made (or will now make) a faithful commitment to joyfully, regularly, generously and sacrificially give my time, talents, and treasure to [Your Church].

"Bring the whole tithe into the storehouse, that there may be food in my house. Test me in this, says the Lord Almighty, and see if I will not open the floodgates of heaven and pour out so much blessing that you will not have room for it." (Malachi 3:10)

_____ I realize that the Biblical pattern of leadership is by example. I will strive to be of a humble spirit, speaking in patience and love, following the example of Jesus. I will never ask of others what I am unwilling to do myself.

"Here is a trustworthy saying: if anyone sets his heart on being an overseer, he desires a noble task. Now an overseer must be above reproach, the husband of but one wife, temperate, self-controlled, respectable, hospitable,

able to teach, not given to drunkenness, not violent but gentle, not quarrelsome, not a lover of money."
(1 Timothy 3:1-3)

"Don't let anyone look down on you because you are young, but set an example for the believers in speech, in life, in faith, and in purity." (1 Timothy 4:12)

"Do not rebuke an older man harshly, but exhort him as if he were your father. Treat younger men as brothers, older women as mothers, and younger women as sisters, with absolute purity." (1 Timothy 5:1-2)

_____ I will support the staff at [Your Church] by my behavior, prayers, and presence. I will not speak ill of them to others but will bring any concerns I have directly to their attention.

"If your brother sins against you, go and show him his fault, just between the two of you ..." (Matthew 18:15)

"I urge you, brothers and sisters, by our Lord Jesus Christ and by the love of the Spirit, to join with me in my struggle by praying to God for me." (Romans 15:30)

_____ I understand that I am called to serve those I lead and that this servanthood is essentially in matters spiritual, bringing the Good News of Jesus Christ to others and doing my part to live healthy and vibrantly in accordance with the Gospel. I commit myself to these biblical standards because I want the best for the Body of Christ at [Your Church].

"The King will reply, I tell you the truth, whatever you did for the least of these, you did for me." (Matthew 25:40)

I agree with and am in compliance to each of the points above.

_____

Signature   Date

KEY TOOL:
Vision Convergence Worksheet

Discerning vision is of the utmost importance for pastors and leaders. But how do you go about it? Where do you even start? The Vision Convergence Worksheet[38] helps surface vision through identifying our passions, ways in which we see God at work, and perceived gaps between what is and what should be – in our community, church, and leaders. Take time to pray and work through the worksheet, following the steps below:

1. Using the diagram that follows, list passion areas for your community, church, and leaders. For example, if your surrounding community is known for after-school youth programs, list it. If your congregation is passionate about small group fellowship with one another, list it. If your leaders are passionate about being incarnational in the community, list it. When you are complete, note any passions that exist in all three of the circles and list them in the middle of the diagram. Also note any passions that exist in two of the circles, and list them in the overlapping space.

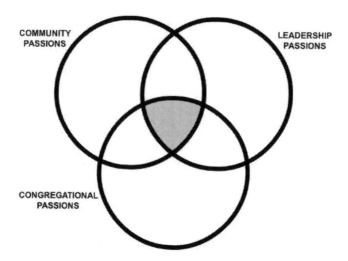

2. List the ways in which you see God clearly working in your community, church, and leaders. When you are complete, note the ways in which God is working in like fashion in all three of the circles and list them in the middle of the diagram. Also note the ways in which God is working in like fashion in two of the circles, and list them in the overlapping space.

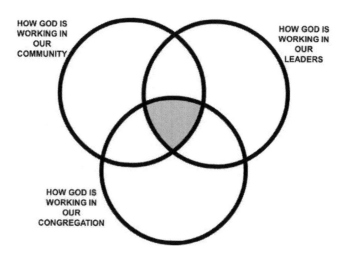

3. List some significant gaps between what is and what should be in your community, church, and leaders. Is poverty worse in your community than what you believe to be acceptable? Does your church struggle with apathy? Are your leaders disengaged from core ministries? Whatever you believe the gaps to be, list them, but be sure that the gaps you are discontented about bring discontent to God as well. When you are complete, note common gaps that are listed in all three of the circles and list them in the middle of the diagram. Also note any like gaps that exist in two of the circles, and list them in the overlapping space.

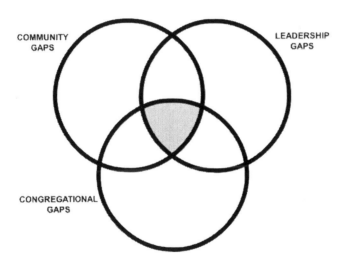

4. Look to identify convergence between passion, ways in which we see God at work, and gaps. Where passion aligns with ways in which God is clearly at work, consider how you might cooperate. Where passion aligns with gaps, consider how you might help bridge the gap. The more convergence there is, the higher the likelihood that you have identified aspects of vision.

KEY TOOL:
S.W.O.T. Analysis Template

The S.W.O.T. Analysis is a commonly used, widely accepted tool that is effective for identifying strengths, weaknesses, opportunities and threats relative to a given project or organization. The tool has been used for many years, and while its origins are unknown, many have credited Albert S. Humphrey with developing S.W.O.T. in the 1960s.

I have found the S.W.O.T. Analysis to be effective as a means of identifying what is and what could be, and as a catalyst for identifying ways in which the gaps between what is and what could be might be bridged.

The process is simple and straightforward. Begin by gathering your leaders together, and brainstorming thoughts relative to each of the four areas.

> ➤ For *Strengths*, capture what your church does well, what and who your key resources are, and what others in the congregation and/or community would likely see as your strengths.
> ➤ For *Weaknesses*, consider ways in which the church can improve. Be sure to capture where you lack resources, and to project how visitors might initially assess the church.
> ➤ For *Opportunities*, think about how you might leverage your strengths into opportunities, and conversely how your weaknesses might be overcome through fresh

opportunities. Consider also where you see God already at work, and how you might join God as you go forward.

> For *Threats*, list ways in which the church might be vulnerable in some manner. If a weakness also represents a threat, capture it accordingly.

Again, bear in mind that the S.W.O.T. Analysis is simply to help inform what is (strengths and weaknesses) and what could be (opportunities), as well as surfacing threats to be aware of. The tool does not in itself produce long-range plans, objectives, strategies, or ministry/department plans, but is useful for spurring deeper thinking as the planning process moves along.

Strengths What do we do well? What/who are our key resources? What do others see as our strengths?	Weaknesses Where can we improve? Where are we lacking in resources? What do others see as our weaknesses?
Opportunities What opportunities are open to us? What trends could we take advantage of? How can we turn our strengths into opportunities?	Threats What threats could harm us? What threats do our weaknesses expose us to?

KEY TOOL:
"Here to There" Template

One of the most impactful leadership lessons I have ever received came from Bill Hybels at the 2010 Willow Creek Global Leadership Summit. Hybels talked about the foundational need for leaders to move people (and organizations) from "here to there." He shared that he used to think that the first step in casting a white hot vision was to describe how great things would be when the church arrived "there," but eventually discovered that most people preferred the comfort of "here" over the uncertainty of "there." Hybels explained that for many years his response to congregational apathy was to crank up the vision even higher, assuming that people would eventually come around to it. But then came the profound realization that for most people, a vision in itself is not enough to compel individuals and organizations to change. Rather, Hybels explained, our first play must not be to make "there" sound wonderful, but to convey the slow death of staying "here." He pointed out that before Martin Luther King Jr. gave his "I have a dream" speech, he gave hundreds of "we can't stay here" speeches.

As leaders, we need to take stock of what was, cooperate with God for what is, and seek God's leading for what could be. Looking back, looking around, and looking forward is paramount.

The tool below is a simple template to help you understand

what it might entail to move from "here" (what is) to "there" (what could be). The tool focuses on essential church-wide considerations rather than specific ministries or departments. The process is straightforward, but be sure to make your descriptions brief and to the point - summary level rather than detailed.

For each of the categories listed on the far left-hand side …

➢ *Describe "Here" (what is).* Consider the present in light of the past; are you in a better place, a worse place, or about the same place as you were a year ago? Consider also the ways you see God at work.

➢ *Describe "There" (what could be).* How do you sense God is leading you? How might cooperating with where God is already working inform "there."

➢ *Consider what moving from "here' to "there" might entail.* What might you need to do differently? What sacrifices might need to be made? What priorities might need to shift?

Set your work aside, but keep it handy as you move into Annual Planning. And don't forget to keep praying and seeking after God's will and leading!

	"HERE" *(what is)*	"THERE" *(what could be)*	What might it entail to move from "HERE" to "THERE?"
Mission Attainment (bringing people to Christ; helping people grow to be more like Christ)			
Vision Acuity (having a clear understanding of vision; stepping toward the vision)			
Values Adherence (understanding core values, and functioning in accordance)			
Walking by Faith (trusting in God and willing to follow where He leads ... decisions marked by faith rather than fear or fact)			
Rooted in Love (a clear, growing love for God and people that marks the church)			
Committed to Prayer (a steadfast commitment to prayer that permeates the church, its ministries, and its people)			
Spirit & Truth Worship (corporate worship marked by biblical truth and movement of the Holy Spirit)			
"All In" Discipleship (all persons are encouraged to be discipled while helping disciple others)			
Honest Fellowship (people connecting with one another in Christ-centered, honest relationships)			
Shared Outreach (fully committed to teaching, equipping, and challenging members to bring the Gospel to the lost)			
Gift-Based Service (helping members understand their spiritual gifts, talents, and passions, and serving in accordance)			

KEY TOOL:
Solid-Slushy-Liquid Template

The *"Solid-Slushy-Liquid" Template* is a tool to identify plans to implement in the coming year ("solid"), plans to target in the coming year that may carry into the following year ("slushy"), and plans that are not feasible in the next few years but merit holding on to ("liquid"). The tool is typically used in annual planning when prioritizing potential objectives during *Deliberation*.

1. Using the first template that follows, begin by listing all potential objectives.

2. Using the 1-5 scale shown, enter a score in each column for each objective.

   a. For 'Mission Impact,' ask, "What is the likelihood of this objective helping us to reach more people for Christ? What is the likelihood of this objective helping people to be more like Christ?"

   b. For 'Resources,' ask, "What is the likelihood that we will have adequate financial resources to implement this objective? What is the likelihood that we will have the 'right' people in place to implement this objective? What is the likelihood that our leadership team will have the capacity to *fully* commit to pursuing this objective?"

c. For 'Feasibility,' ask, "What is the likelihood of achieving this objective *this year*? What is the likelihood of achieving this objective *next year*? What is the likelihood of achieving this objective in 3+ *years*?

POTENTIAL OBJECTIVES:	MISSION IMPACT		RESOURCES			FEASIBILITY		
	REACH PEOPLE	GROW PEOPLE	FINANCIAL	PEOPLE	LEADERSHIP CAPACITY	LIKELIHOOD OF SUCCESS THIS YEAR	LIKELIHOOD OF SUCCESS NEXT YEAR	LIKELIHOOD OF SUCCESS IN 3+ YEARS

Use the scale below to enter a score in each column for each potential objective.

5 Excellent
4 Good
3 Average
2 Below Average
1 Well Below Average

3. After completing the template above, take time to analyze what you have entered. Think and pray about how best to go forward. Remember, your task is to narrow your objectives, along with their accompanying strategies, to no more than five. As you gain clarity, use the template below to plot your objectives in the category – solid, slushy, or liquid – that you deem most appropriate.

SOLID (implement in the coming year)	SLUSHY (target this year; be open to moving to next year)	LIQUID (Do not implement now; reconsider in 2-3 years)

KEY TOOL:
Annual Planning Retreat Template

I had the joy and privilege of working alongside Pastor Eric Cook during the 3+ years I served at Remembrance Church in Grand Rapids, Michigan. Eric possesses many outstanding ministry gifts and talents, but near the top of the list is his ability to structure and lead a weekend planning retreat. While the template that follows is one that I have created, it is strongly influenced by Rev. Cook. The template offers a solid framework that leaves space for you to personalize your retreat for your church leadership team. May the Lord bless you and your team as you discern together what the Lord is calling you to pursue in the coming year!

DAY/FOCUS		TIME	ACTIVITY	WHAT TO PLAN FOR IN ADVANCE			
FRIDAY	CALIBRATION	6:00 PM 7:15 PM	Arrival; check-in; dinner	Retreat dates and location	Lodging	Meals and snacks	
		7:15 PM 7:30 PM	Welcome and brief overview of the weekend	Packets for leaders	Audio, video	Room arrangement	
		7:30 PM 8:00 PM	Prayer and worship ("look up")	Worship leader	Song sheets or projector		
		8:00 PM 8:45 PM	Teaching and Discussion ("look back; look around")	Devotional leader	Scripture that informs current reality		
		8:45 PM 9:00 PM	Closing Prayer				
SATURDAY	IDEATION	8:00 AM 9:00 AM	Breakfast				
		9:00 AM 10:00 AM	Prayer, worship, devotion, instructions for ideation	Devotional leader	Scripture that informs current reality		
		10:00 AM Noon	Ideation	Facilitator	Room arrangement	Supplies, etc.	
	DELIBERATION	Noon 2:30 PM	Lunch/Open Time … while sub-team prioritizes ideas	Categorization sub-team	Quiet time for team to work	Activities for leaders	
		2:30 PM 2:45 PM	Prayer and worship				
		2:45 PM 3:00 PM	Sub-team gives summary of work, presenting possible objectives/strategies	Approach for reporting			
		3:00 PM 5:30 PM	Deliberation process	Completed Faith-Based tools available			
	VALIDATION	5:30 PM 7:30 PM	Dinner, open time				
		7:30 PM 7:45 PM	Prayer, revisit results of deliberation				
		7:45 PM 8:30 PM	Validation process	F.A.I.T.H. Filter			
SUNDAY	CONSECRATION	8:00 AM 9:00 AM	Breakfast				
		9:00 AM 10:00 AM	Worship service for leaders, with Communion	Communion elements			
		10:00 AM 10:15 AM	Wrap-up, clean-up	Clean-up crew	Communicate next steps		

KEY TOOL:
Keep-Alter-Add-Stop Template

The Keep-Alter-Stop-Add tool is useful for discerning Ministry/Department Plans. The detailed instructions were provided in the Ministry/Department Plans chapter, and accompany the template provided here.

	INVENTORY	KEEP	ALTER	STOP	ADD	EXPLANATION	EST. COST
CURRENT	Example A		X			Changing curriculuum to better align with objective #1	$2,500
	Example B	X				This event is essential for the ministry and is working well	$4,000
	Example C			X		This event no longer aligns with our vision and is being stopped	($1,500)
NEW	Example D				X	Offsite class to help volunteers understand and teach from the new curriculuum	$500

KEY TOOL:

Annual Ministry Plan Template

The Annual Ministry Plan is an essential document to share how God has led, and is leading, your church. In essence the plan writes itself, since its content has largely already been completed! The template below is intended to be used as a booklet. The booklet approach works well, and the template will help you to capture essential content, but if you want your Ministry Plan to really stand out I recommend contracting with a creative, skilled graphic artist who will bring it to a whole new level. Hiring a professional to help communicate a well discerned, Holy Spirit led plan is much more of an investment than it is an expense.

Annual Ministry Plan Template:
Front Cover

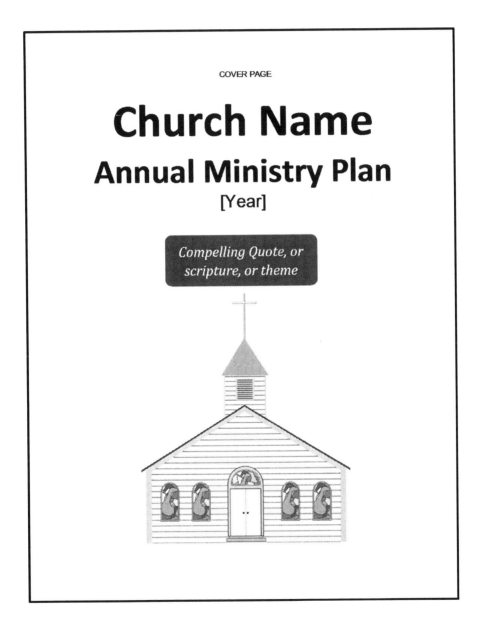

COVER PAGE

Church Name
Annual Ministry Plan
[Year]

Compelling Quote, or scripture, or theme

Annual Ministry Plan Template:
Inside Flap (Page 2)

Contents:

Who We Are and What We Believe:
Brief summary of the church - just a short paragraph.

Our Mission:
List your mission statement here.

Our Vision:
List your vision statement here. If your vision is directional, give a general idea of how you sense God leading the church.

Our Values:
Before listing your values, mention that the values listed here represent what the church stands for, and will safeguard through all circumstances, and all times.

Annual Ministry Plan Template:

Page 3

PAGE 3

Faith-Based Planning
This is the place to provide a brief summary of the process you used for planning. Use what I have written, or express the approach in your own words – the choice is yours.

Why We Plan
Planning helps us to avoid making hasty decisions that lead to poverty – to ruin:
"The plans of the diligent lead to profit as surely as haste leads to poverty." (Proverbs 21:5)

Even as we plan, we are intentional to submit our plans to the Lord:
"Commit to the Lord whatever you do, and your plans will succeed." (Proverbs 16:3)

Finally, we commit to holding our plans loosely, knowing that God's purpose prevails:
"Many are the plans in a man's heart, but it is the Lord's purpose that prevails" (Prov. 19:21)

How We Plan
Over the past X months, the leaders at [your church] have worked through a comprehensive planning process called *Faith-Based*. We have spent considerable time praying, reflecting, and seeking to discern what God has in store for us. This plan is the product of our journey. We are excited about how God is leading us, and invite you to join us on the journey – to the glory of God!

The diagram below illustrates the six cycles of *Faith-Based*. In the pages that follow, we'll share what we learned in each phase, and how we arrived at the plans we have identified.

The F.A.I.T.H. Filter
Before we finalized our plans, we examined them on multiple occasions through the F.A.I.T.H. Filter. The filter helps to ensure that our plans are:

Flexible...held loosely; able to be changed as the Lord leads us.

Aligned...with Scripture, our mission, our objectives, RCA "Transformed/Transforming" plan.

Intertwined...synergized and cohesive so that our plans represent a plan.

Transformational...so that lives are changed by the grace and truth of Jesus Christ.

Holy...set apart to God, consecrated to God; surrendered to God.

PAGE 4

Annual Ministry Plan Template:
Page 4

PAGE 4

Preparation

Begin with a brief explanation of the Preparation Phase. Use what follows, or feel free to communicate as you see fit.

The first step in *Faith-Based* was to prepare our hearts and minds. We reaffirmed the supremacy of Christ, and the centrality of the Gospel. We spent time in prayer, and did our best to "be still" and trust that God would guide us through the process. We adopted the alignment model that follows:

God's Great Commission and Great Commandment: God's Great Commission and Commandment are fixed - unchanging. All of our plans must align with and support God's Great Commission and Commandment.

↓↑

Mission: The mission answers the question of why we exist. It equates to God's call – God's purpose – for the church, and comes directly from the Great Commission given us by Christ. Leadership must revisit and recast the mission often to ensure ongoing focus and attainment.

↓↑

Vision: The vision answers the question of what God is leading us to be in the future to fulfill the mission, and when we project (or at least hope) the vision will come to fruition. Vision is at times more directional than specific, but at all times is a sort of picture of how we sense God leading and calling us going forward. Leadership must not only cast the vision, but lead the way in living in accordance with the vision.

↓↑

Values: Our values answer the question of what we will endeavor to safeguard in and through all circumstances and at all times. In essence, our values are what define us; what make us who we are. Values should be over-arching rather than tactical or situational. Values should be revisited annually to either reaffirm or adjust.

↓↑

Long-Range Plans (LRPs): LRPs serve as a bridge between the vision, which is typically 5-7 years from coming to fruition, and objectives, which are established annually. LRPs require at least 2 years, and as many as 5 years, to complete. Establishing LRPs is optional during the planning cycle, but if LRPs exist, they should be revisted and reassessed annually.

↓↑

Objectives: Objectives answer the question of what God is leading us to do in the coming year to be faithful to the mission, step toward the vision, and uphold our values. Objectives are established annually, communicated regularly and creatively to the congregation, and should be at least somewhat measurable. Objectives must *clearly* align with mission, vision, and values.

↓↑

Strategies: Strategies answer the question of what we will do in the coming year to achieve the objectives. Typically, strategies are set annually in conjunction with establishing objectives. Strategies can be altered, stopped, or added throughout the year as the Holy Spirit leads and guides.

↓↑

Ministry/Department Plans: Ministry/Department Plans are the individual plans from each of our ministries and departments. These plans are typically set by staff and answer the question of how our ministries and departments, in the coming year, will help fulfill the mission, step toward the vision, and support the objectives and strategies.

↓↑

Tactics: Tactics are fluid - ever-changing - and essential for success. Tactics are ways in which we try to optimize success against objectives, strategies, and ministry/department plans. Tactics change often based on how the Spirit leads, and what is taking place in and around us.

↓↑

HR Plan: The HR Plan delineates people, positions, and responsibilities. The HR Plan should represent what we believe to be optimal stewardship of the staff (and possibly key volunteers) that God has brought to us. Most often, the HR Plan entails minor adjustments to position and/or job scope, but at times more significant changes are necessary.

↓↑

Budget: The budget must align with and support all that we do. The budget must be developed with ample prayer and steadfast commitment to good stewardship. The budget, as with all of our plans, must be "faith-based" and held loosely.

Annual Ministry Plan Template:

Page 5

PAGE 5

Assessment

Explain that a key aspect of Holy Spirit led planning is to take an honest look at who we are as a church. Place special emphasis on the church's current ability to reach people for Christ, and to help people grow to be more like Christ. Here, honesty and transparency are what is required.

If you had an annual plan in place last year, it is appropriate to provide an objective assessment of how you fared against the plan. The scorecard below is effective for communicating a summary level progress report.

Review of Last Year's Objectives & Strategies

Throughout the year, we use a Green-Yellow-Red scorecard to track how we're doing against objectives and strategies. The scorecard is complete for [fiscal year]:

[YOUR] Church - [FISCAL YEAR] Scorecard				Update as of [DATE]
Objectives and Strategies	Target Date	Status	Update	Actions to be taken this month
Sample Objective: Develop and implement a means for identifying and developing emerging leaders	12/31	SLIGHT RISK	As shown by the updates below, good progress has been made overall. However, the fourth strategy will require intervention from the Board of Elders.	In addition to the actions listed below for each strategy, we are planning on visiting Eastside Church to learn more about what they're doing in this area.
First strategy: Bring in a consultant to train staff and leaders on how to identify and encourage emerging leaders	2/28	COMPLETE	John Doe from XYZ Consulting trained our staff and leaders on 2/15	N/A
Second strategy: Introduce a monthly "lunch and learn" for emerging leaders	4/30	SLIGHT RISK	The first lunch was poorly attended. Several mentioned that they are not able to get out of work for an hour during the workday.	We are planning on shifting the next session to a Saturday morning breakfast
Third strategy: Pilot a mentoring program to match mature, seasoned leaders with young, emerging leaders	7/31	ON TRACK	We have made great progress on curriculum options and have enlisted 8 people who are willing to serve as mentors	We are sending a letter, to be followed up with a personal contact, to 12 people who have been targeted as a potential emerging leader
Fourth strategy: Begin to selectively integrate emerging leaders into ministry teams	11/30	HIGH RISK	This is a concern at this time. Many people who are currently serving on ministry teams are wary of bringing in younger leaders	We have asked for a meeting with the Board of Elders to get their input. Without giving emerging leaders opportunities to serve, this objective will be unrealized

Annual Ministry Plan Template:

Page 6

The second page in the Assessment section should convey specific information relative to completed assessment. If you did an outside assessment, or the first Spiritual Farming template, or the Deep and Wide exercise, summarize your findings on this page.

Spiritual Farming

In the Assessment phase, we studied the Parable of the Sower in order to consider the climate, roots, and soil of our church. What we discovered is ...

The **climate** at our church is generally [describe]. This means that [describe].
The **roots** of our church are generally [describe]. This means that [describe].
Based on our climate and roots, we believe that our pace of change should be [describe].

The **soil** at our church is generally [describe]. This means that [describe].
We believe that our soil might bear more fruit if we [describe].

We believe that the **seed** we sow is [describe].This means that [describe].
Some ideas we have to sow better seed are [describe].

Deep and Wide

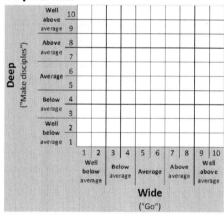

The mission that Christ has given us both wide ("Go") and deep ("make disciples"). Using a simple 1-10 scale, our leaders gave an honest assessment of where they believe we are today relative to both aspects of the Great Commission. The results are shown at left.

As shown, our belief is that we are X in the "wide" dimension, and X in the "deep" dimension. All told, our assessment is that we are achieving around X% of what is possible for our church. We are energized by the possibility of making strides in each aspect that will have major impact.

Annual Ministry Plan Template:

Page 7

Long-Range Planning

Begin by giving a brief summary of the approach you took to affirm, or revise, mission, vision, and values. You may also elect to summarize key findings/learnings.

Additionally, if you completed the Vision Convergence Worksheet, or S.W.O.T. Analysis, or "Here to There" template, consider providing a summary of your work.

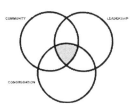

Vision Convergence Exercise

The Vision Convergence exercise led us to consider what our community, church, and leaders are most passionate about, followed by listing ways we see God working in those passion areas, and identifying gaps between what is, and what should be. The exercise identified areas of overlap between passion, where we see God at work, and gaps. Our desire is to cooperate fully with God's leading as we go forward. Here is where we see convergence: [Describe].

Strengths-Weaknesses-Opportunities-Threats (S.W.O.T.) Exercise

We spent time considering our strengths, weaknesses, opportunities and threats in order to better understand where we are today (strengths and weaknesses), where God may be leading us tomorrow (opportunities), and possible barriers to stepping fully into God's plan for us (threats). Here is a summary of our work: [Describe].

"Here to There" Exercise

This exercise helped us to understand what it might take to move from where we are to where we sense God is calling us. The tool is focused on key church-wide considerations rather than specific ministries or departments, and was useful as we began to discern objectives and strategies. Here is a summary of our findings: [Describe].

Annual Ministry Plan Template:

Page 8

PAGE 8

Annual Planning

Our leaders used a five-step annual planning process to discern objectives and strategies. The process is summarized here:

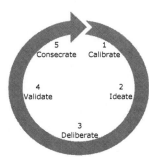

Step 1: Calibrate. Before putting pen to paper, we took time to fix our focus on God rather than ourselves.

Step 2: Ideate. Here we listed a variety of ideas for consideration.

Step 3: Deliberate. In the deliberation step, we scrutinized, categorized, and prioritized ideas in order to begin firming up plans.

Step 4: Validate. Before locking in objectives and strategies, we paused to make sure that they were aligned with and supportive of our mission, vision, and values.

Step 5: Consecrate. We surrendered our work to God!

Objectives and Strategies

Provide a sentence or two to convey any sort of theme that emerged from your objectives and strategies, then list them below.

Objective 1: [Describe].

> Strategy 1.a: [Describe].

> Strategy 1.b: [Describe].

> Strategy 1.c: [Describe].

Objective 2: [Describe].

> Strategy 2.a: [Describe].

> Strategy 2.b: [Describe].

> Strategy 2.c: [Describe].

Annual Ministry Plan Template:
Page 9

PAGE 9

Alignment

Briefly describe the importance of aligning Ministry/Department plans, staffing, governance, and budget with the church's mission, vision, objectives and strategies.

Ministry/Department Plans

Describe the process used to create Ministry/Department Plans. Use the following, or express your approach using your own words:

Our ministry and department leaders used a ""Keep-Alter-Stop-Add" process to discern ministries, programs, and events that should continue as is (keep), need to be changed in some manner (alter), have run their course (stop), or need to be added to the mix (add). The grid below summarizes what we will be changing, stopping, or adding:

Ministry 1:
      Changing: [describe]
      Stopping: [Describe]
      Adding [Describe]

Ministry 2:
      Changing: [describe]
      Stopping: [Describe]
      Adding [Describe]

Ministry 3:
      Changing: [describe]
      Stopping: [Describe]
      Adding [Describe]

Ministry 4:
      Changing: [describe]
      Stopping: [Describe]
      Adding [Describe]

Department 1:
      Changing: [describe]
      Stopping: [Describe]
      Adding [Describe]

Department 2:
      Changing: [describe]
      Stopping: [Describe]
      Adding [Describe]

Annual Ministry Plan Template:
Page 10

Adding [Describe]

PAGE 10

General Budget

Before presenting the budget, consider conveying a few key stewardship points that remind others that everything belongs to the Lord, we trust God for His provision, etc.

Next, provide a budget summary in whatever format your church prefers. I recommend that you resist the temptation to list each and every line item. Instead, provide a categorical, summary-level budget. For those who want all of the detail, make it available, but don't list in the Annual Ministry Plan

Briefly summarize the budget:

The leadership at [your church] is proposing a general budget for [fiscal year] of $X, which equates to a X% decrease/increase. Some key considerations in forming the budget are [describe].

Contingency Plan

After the budget summary, inform readers that the leadership, in trusting the Lord for what He will provide through His people, have identified contingency actions in the event that giving is significantly less than budgeted, and significantly more than budget. Feel free to list some of the contingency plan details, especially as it relates to over and above gifts helping the church to pursue its vision and long-range plans.

Annual Ministry Plan Template:
Page 11

Execution

Describe how the church will work to do all it can to make good on the plans that the Holy Spirit has led the church to pursue.

Be sure to touch on your use of Monthly Scorecards

As you close the plan, express thanks and praise to God for His call, leading, and provision.

Annual Ministry Plan Template:
Page 12 (Back Cover)

PAGE 12 (BACK PAGE)

Consider placing an inspiring graphic here, in addition to your address, phone, web address, etc.

KEY TOOL:
Scorecard Template

Amonthly scorecard for reporting progress of objectives and strategies is essential. The template below is a simple yet effective tool. While the illustration below is in grayscale, I recommend using a color-coded scorecard for the status column, with the key as follows:

Blue: Complete

Green: On track to complete on time

Yellow: Moderately at risk based on current status

Blue: Significantly at risk, not likely to be completed.

[YOUR] Church - [FISCAL YEAR] Scorecard				Update as of [DATE]
Objectives and Strategies	**Target Date**	**Status**	**Update**	**Actions to be taken this month**
Sample Objective: Develop and implement a means for identifying and developing emerging leaders	12/31	SLIGHT RISK	As shown by the updates below, good progress has been made overall. However, the fourth strategy will require intervention from the Board of Elders.	In addition to the actions listed below for each strategy, we are planning on visiting Eastside Church to learn more about what they're doing in this area.
First strategy: Bring in a consultant to train staff and leaders on how to identify and encourage emerging leaders.	2/28	COMPLETE	John Doe from XYZ Consulting trained our staff and leaders on 2/15.	N/A
Second strategy: Introduce a monthly 'lunch and learn" for emerging leaders.	4/30	SLIGHT RISK	The first lunch was poorly attended. Several mentioned that they are not able to get out of work for an hour during the workday.	We are planning on shifting the next session to a Saturday morning breakfast.
Third strategy: Pilot a mentoring program to match mature, seasoned leaders with young, emerging leaders.	7/31	ON TRACK	We have made great progress on curriculum options, and have enlisted 8 people who are willing to serve as mentors.	We are sending a letter, to be followed up with a personal contact, to 12 people who have been targeted as a potential emerging leader.
Fourth strategy: Begin to selectively integrate emerging leaders into ministry teams.	11/30	HIGH RISK	This is a concern at this time. Many people who are currently serving on ministry teams are wary of bringing in younger leaders.	We have asked for a meeting with the Board of Elders to get their input. Without giving emerging leaders opportunities to serve, this objective will be unrealized.

APPENDIX A

ADVANCING THE GOSPEL IN THE FIRST CENTURY: LESSONS FROM PAUL'S FIRST MISSIONARY JOURNEY

Recorded in Acts 13-14, Paul's first missionary journey highlights the importance of planning, and how to go about planning.

We begin by considering the foundations of Paul's faith, and the clarity of Paul's call. Having studied under the esteemed Rabbi Gamaliel, Paul knew the scriptures up and down. But like many others in his day, Paul was blind to the truth of Jesus Christ, who represented the fulfillment of the very scriptures Paul based his life on. All of this changed during a journey to Damascus, when Paul's eyes were shut physically but opened spiritually. Subsequently, Paul made clear that Jesus personally gave him the Gospel, along with clarity on what to do with the Gospel:

> "I want you to know, brothers and sisters, that the gospel I preached is not of human origin. I did not receive it from any man, nor was I taught it; rather, I received it by revelation from Jesus Christ." (Galatians 1:11-12)

"However, I consider my life worth nothing to me; my only aim is to finish the race and complete the task the Lord Jesus has given me — the task of testifying to the good news of God's grace." (Acts 20:24)

Paul was given a **mission** from Jesus Himself: To spread the Good News of the Gospel.

Even as Paul was anchored in the truth of the Gospel, and committed to his mission call of spreading the Gospel, Jesus gave him still more clarity on how he was to fulfill his mission:

"Now get up and stand on your feet. I have appeared to you to appoint you as a servant and as a witness of what you have seen and will see of me. I will rescue you from your own people and from the Gentiles. I am sending you to them to open their eyes and turn them from darkness to light, and from the power of Satan to God, so that they may receive forgiveness of sins and a place among those who are sanctified by faith in me." (Acts 26:16-18)

The **vision** that Jesus gave Paul was to bring the Gospel message of salvation to *all* people. How stunning this vision must have been to Paul, a "son of Pharisees" (Acts 23:6), a "Hebrew of Hebrews" (Phil. 3:5)! Yet Paul did not waiver. Rather, anchored in the saving truth of the Gospel, Paul spent his remaining years living out the vision he received from Christ.

"I am not ashamed of the gospel, because it is the power of God that brings salvation to everyone who believes: first to the Jew, then to the Gentile." (Romans 1:16)

After his conversion, Paul immediately began to preach in Damascus, but left after a short time to spend three years in Arabia calibrating his heart and mind to God (Gal. 1:15-18). After a brief time in Jerusalem, Paul faced intense persecution and was forced to flee for his life. He set sail from Caesarea to his birth place of Tarsus, where he spent around four years preaching and teaching in the surrounding regions of Syria and Cilicia. Eventually, because of the rapid growth of the church at Antioch in Syria, Barnabas found Paul and brought him to Antioch (Acts 11:25).

> "So for a whole year Barnabas and Saul met with the church and taught great numbers of people. The disciples were called Christians first at Antioch." (Acts 11:26)

Long before they were sent out by the church in Antioch, Paul invested in the church – meeting with and teaching "great numbers" of people. In essence, what he and Barnabas were doing is calibrating themselves, and the church as a whole, to the things of God.

After a year in Antioch, Paul and Barnabas traveled to Jerusalem to help the Judean believers. Upon their return to Antioch (and undoubtedly during their absence), the leaders of the Antioch church met to worship, fast, and pray for the leading of the Holy Spirit:

> "Now in the church at Antioch there were prophets and teachers: Barnabas, Simeon called Niger, Lucius of Cyrene, Manaen (who had been brought up with Herod the tetrarch) and Saul. While they were worshiping the Lord

and fasting, the Holy Spirit said, 'Set apart for me Barnabas and Saul for the work to which I have called them.' So after they had fasted and prayed, they placed their hands on them and sent them off." (Acts 13:1-3)

The Antioch leaders understood that before looking ahead, they needed to look up – *"worshiping the Lord and fasting."*

Even after hearing from the Holy Spirit, sending Paul and Barnabas took great faith on the part of the Antioch leaders. Their preference may have been to receive detailed instructions, but what they received instead was a vague call, to "set apart for me Barnabas and Saul for the work to which I have called them." For the faithful leaders at Antioch, this was enough, and so after fasting and praying, they placed their hands on Paul and Barnabas and sent them off.

There is little question that as they set sail for Cyprus, Paul and Barnabas, undergirded by the prayers of their sending church, continued to calibrate their minds and hearts to God - "looking up" in prayer and worship, and "looking back" while meditating on the scriptures. Upon their arrival, they began to "look around," proclaiming the word of God in synagogues (Acts 13:5).

When we truly commit to calibrating ourselves to God, we can expect the unexpected. Paul and Barnabas traveled through the entire island until coming to Paphos, where the proconsul sent for them out of a desire to hear the word of God. However, a Jewish sorcerer/false prophet named Bar-Jesus (also interpreted as Elymas) opposed them and tried to steer the proconsul from the faith. Paul, in an ironic twist, pronounced blindness on Elymus, which came to pass. Hence, the proconsul believed, "amazed at the teaching of the Lord." (Acts 13:12)

For Paul and Barnabas, the incident in Paphos marked a significant change in their ministry. Before Paphos, they are referred to in scripture as "Barnabas and Saul" (Acts 11:26, 11:30, 12:25, 13:2, 13:7); after Paphos, they are referred to as "Paul and Barnabas" (Acts 13:42, 13:43, 13:46, 13:50, 14:1, 14:3, 14:23, 15:2, 15:22, 15:35, 15:36). In other words, whereas Barnabas had been recognized as the senior leader, Paul – no longer referred to as Saul – would now serve in that capacity. Both leaders were called to the mission at hand, but delineating their respective roles allowed each to thrive, functioning out of their specific call and giftedness.

This is a significant lesson for today's church. While it's important to get the right people on the bus, it's equally important to help them find the right seat. Much of the turnover in our churches comes from good people on the wrong bus, or occupying the wrong seat.

While scripture does not detail how Paul came to develop a strategic plan, there is little question that over the course of time he did just that. And while the terms "objectives" and "strategies" are nowhere to be found in scripture, there is ample scriptural evidence that the inspiration of the Holy Spirit, combined with Paul's personal experience and growing understanding of his call, led to pronounced strategic clarity for Paul.

Having been sent by the Holy Spirit (Acts 13:4), Paul trusted this same Holy Spirit to lead him. But Paul understood that patience did not equate to passivity, and that active ministry was essential for strategic clarity. When Paul and Barnabas arrived in Pisidian Antioch (in Asia Minor, not Syria), they did what they always did – they visited the local synagogue. Once again their faithfulness was rewarded:

"After the reading from the Law and the Prophets, the leaders of the synagogue sent word to them, saying, 'Brothers, if you have a word of exhortation for the people, please speak.'" (Acts 13:15)

Paul begins by "looking back," recounting the exodus of the Jewish people from Egypt and the ascension of David to the throne (Acts 13:16-22). Paul continues by "looking around," connecting David's lineage to the coming of Jesus Christ, in whom the "message of salvation has been sent" (Acts 13:26), and through whom "everyone who believes is set free from every sin" (Acts 13:39).

As Paul and Barnabas left the synagogue in Pisidian Antioch, "the people invited them to speak further about these things on the next Sabbath. When the congregation was dismissed, many of the Jews and devout converts to Judaism followed Paul and Barnabas, who talked with them and urged them to continue in the grace of God." (Acts 13:42-43)

The next week, nearly the whole city gathered to hear the word of God. Predictably, many Jews grew jealous and began to verbally abuse Paul, to which he and Barnabas boldly replied:

"We had to speak the word of God to you first. Since you reject it and do not consider yourselves worthy of eternal life, we now turn to the Gentiles." (Acts 13:46)

Many of the Gentiles who were appointed to eternal life believed, and the word of the Lord spread through the whole region. Even as Paul and Barnabas were expelled, the "disciples were filled with joy and with the Holy Spirit." (Acts 13:52)

What took place in Paphos, and in Pisidian Antioch, set a course for what would take place in Iconium, where Paul and Barnabas "spoke so effectively that a great number of Jews and Greeks believed" (Acts 14:1). With their roles established, their gifts exercised, and their hearts ablaze, Paul and Barnabas continued their mission.

After learning of a plot to stone them, Paul and Barnabas traveled to Lystra, where Paul was stoned and dragged out of the city, given up for dead. Remarkably, after the disciples gathered around him, he returned to the city to finish what he had started!

Before completing their journey, Paul and Barnabas returned to Lystra, Iconium and Antioch, "strengthening the disciples and encouraging them to remain true to the faith." (Acts 14:22)

Paul's first missionary journey was instrumental in establishing a strategic plan that he would carry out for the remainder of his years. Strategic clarity was forged through the intersection of Holy Spirit inspiration and personal experience. And while Paul didn't list objectives and strategies per se, it is clear that he had a plan, which was essentially this:

Mission: *To spread the Good News of the Gospel.*

Vision: *To bring the Gospel message of salvation to all people.*

Objective 1: *Start Churches.*

> **Strategy 1.a**: *Preach in synagogues whenever possible.*
> Paul embraced the built-in opportunity of sharing the Gospel with Jews and "God fearing" Gentiles in synagogues everywhere he traveled.

"At Iconium Paul and Barnabas went as usual into the Jewish synagogue." (Acts 14:1)

Strategy 1.b: *Contextualized preaching.*
Paul was intentional to share the Gospel in light of the whole of scripture, demonstrating how what has taken place points to Christ, and what was prophesied has been fulfilled in Christ.

"We tell you the good news: What God promised our ancestors he has fulfilled for us, their children, by raising up Jesus." (Acts 13:32-33)

Strategy 1.c: *Start churches in main cities.*
Paul employed an urban planting strategy to reach as many as possible, trusting that these urban churches would expand their outreach and ministry to rural and surrounding areas.

"Most mission historians believe that the apostle Paul started churches in a major city of each region and then left the region when there was a church established there. He considered a region to be reached when its major city had a church. He knew that the city church would influence the entire region for the gospel and, once established, he could move on to the next place."
From *11 Innovations in the Local Church*, by Elmer Towns, Ed Stetzer, and Warren Bird

Objective 2: *Strengthen Churches.*

Strategy 2.a: *Ongoing Connection.*

"Then they returned to Lystra, Iconium and Antioch ..." (Acts 14:21b)

Strategy 2.b: *Encourage and disciple new believers.*

"...strengthening the disciples and encouraging them to remain true to the faith." (Acts 14:22)

Strategy 2.c: *Mobilize and commission leaders.*

"Paul and Barnabas appointed elders for them in each church and, with prayer and fasting, committed them to the Lord, in whom they had put their trust." (Acts 14:23)

What lessons might your church learn and apply from Paul, Barnabas, and the Antioch church? There is much to be gleaned from Paul's first missionary journey, not least of which is the importance of sharing and celebrating God's faithfulness.

"On arriving there [Antioch], they gathered the church together and reported all that God had done through them and how he had opened a door of faith to the Gentiles. And they stayed there a long time with the disciples." (Acts 14:27-28)

APPENDIX B

ADVANCING THE GOSPEL IN THE 21ST CENTURY: LESSONS FROM A LOCAL CHURCH

May 3, 2015 was a significant day in the life of Beechwood Church in Holland, Michigan. This was the final Sunday at Beechwood for Pastor Jim Lankheet, who was concluding nearly fourteen years of faithful, fruitful ministry there. Though I had transitioned out of Beechwood some three years prior, I was deeply blessed to be present for, and to celebrate with, a pastor and congregation I love dearly.

During his message, Jim reflected on and gave thanks for the powerful, unmistakable movement of God in and through Beechwood Church. As Jim spoke, I joined him in reflecting on, and thanking God for, all that the Lord did during Jim's ministry at Beechwood. And there was much fruit to celebrate: Six church plants (four Latino churches, a Nepali-speaking church, and a church for people and families with developmental disability); 808 first-time professions (between Beechwood and its church plants); 186 adult baptisms (again, between Beechwood and its church plants); and much more.

I thought about how far Beechwood had come since the day I first entered the church in 1998. I thought about the nine years I served with Jim, the first two as a Deacon, the last seven as Executive Director of Ministries. And I thought about what took place in 2006 - *before* our first church plant, *before* we launched a wholeness ministry, *before* we revamped our mission structure and approach, *before* we redesigned our outdoor worship area, *before* we built a lodge to host and help spur a variety of outdoor ministries.

By 2006, Jim had already invested nearly five years calibrating Beechwood's leadership and congregation to the heart of God. And while the seeds that were sown in those early years would eventually bear fruit, Jim understood that patience - trusting the Lord to lead us in *His* time and according to *His* plan - was the order of the day.

The faithfulness of Rev. Lankheet and the leadership at Beechwood was rewarded in 2006, when throughout that year the Lord's call and vision for Beechwood began to crystalize. By the time 2006 gave way to 2007, we had a plan to launch "Opportunities," a three-year journey that would move Beechwood from being a church with potential to being a church on fire and on mission for the cause of Christ.

The year leading up to Opportunities was just as important as the three years spent implementing Opportunities. It was, in essence, the journey before the journey. In January 2006 we established a process to begin discerning long-range plans. The process included an extended time of prayer in which we pledged unity in Christ while seeking the leading of the Holy Spirit ("looking up"); reflection on God's faithfulness to His people and church ("looking back"); and observation of how God was already at work in and around us ("looking around"). This time of calibration was a vital investment for what lie ahead.

As we considered where we were ("here") and where we sensed God leading us ("there"), we began to dream. In March 2006, we invited the congregation to submit ideas for long-range plans. These ideas were taken into account a few weeks later when our leadership team (staff and consistory) went on retreat to calibrate and ideate.

Over the next two months, we spent time deliberating potential plans and, finally, validating proposed plans. As clarity emerged, we consecrated our plans to the Lord, trusting that where God guides, God provides.

Thus, in May 2006 we introduced four long-range plans, believing that each would be a catalyst for life change in Christ. These long-range plans were:

- ✓ Church planting on a regular, cyclical basis;
- ✓ A wholeness ministry to guide people into the fullness of life in Christ;
- ✓ A redesigned outdoor worship area to enable Beechwood to continue reaching people through its summer outdoor worship;
- ✓ Significant property enhancements, including building a lodge, to facilitate the launch of outdoor ministries that would minister to people in the community.

At the same time, we took steps to align our structure and resources with the vision God placed before us. We proposed a new "Executive Elder" role that would allow certain lay leaders to focus more extensively on long-range initiatives; we filled two open staff positions with leaders that we believed would actively support and help bring forth the vision; we revised our budget to align with the vision; and we called a Latino pastor to start a Spanish language church in our community.

By late 2006, we further discerned that to fully step into the "opportunities" God had presented us with we would need to embark on a capital campaign. In March 2007, the "Opportunities" campaign was launched and the rest, as the saying goes, is history ... thanks be to God!

POSTSCRIPT

Looking back at this period of time at Beechwood Church, I believe that there are three important lessons to convey:

First, that every planning season is different, and adaptability is key. This was a unique time in the life of the church. In many ways, God was calling us to venture off-road. Our old ways of doing things would not suffice. We determined to follow God's leading, adapting as we went and cooperating with the Holy Spirit throughout.

Second, that patience and calibration are not to be underestimated. After the Apostle Paul's conversion, he waited around ten years to embark on his first missionary journey. After arriving at Beechwood, Pastor Jim Lankheet waited around five years to begin long-range planning. Yet both Paul and Jim are classic "activators," passionate leaders inclined to action. The patience to calibrate themselves and other leaders to the things of God is admirable and highly instructive.

And thirdly, while our approach to planning must be

adaptable, using a consistent framework for planning is essential. Beechwood's primary focus in 2006 was long-range discernment, but we did not overlook the importance of annual planning. In fact, if anything, the long-range focus helped solidify several annual objectives, including: Adding a new worship service; forming an Outreach Influence Team (based on the *Organic Outreach* series by Kevin Harney); and transitioning from supporting missionaries to partnering with and sending missionaries.

NOTES

1. Churches that are diligent and effective in planning year over year are often able to shorten the planning timeframe. For these churches, preparation and assessment can be combined and completed in one month, long-range planning and annual planning can be completed in one month, and alignment can be completed in one month. But for most churches it is best to allow the cycle to take a full five months.
2. From *The Seven Habits of Highly Effective People*, by Stephen R. Covey. Habit number two is to "Begin with the end in mind."
3. From *Experiencing God: Knowing and Doing the Will of God*, by Henry Blackaby.
4. Adapted from the accountable leadership model presented in *Winning on Purpose*, by John Edmund Kaiser.
5. While the whole of scripture points to the supremacy of Christ, the book of Hebrews is especially poignant in making this point. Specifically, read Hebrews 1:3-4, 7:24-25, and 8:6.
6. From "Christ at the Center," an interview with Michael Horton (by Mark Galli) in *Christianity Today*, November 19, 2009.
7. From "Big Rocks," a Franklin-Covey training video.
8. Job 38:2
9. Job 42:2
10. *Center Church* is a must read for pastors and leaders! Read it slowly and discuss it as you go. In fact, read it twice for good measure.
11. John 4:29
12. From *Study Guide for Mark 4* by David Guzik, at blueletterbible.org
13. Teaching Franklin-Covey Time Management in a corporate setting brought me great joy. There was a simple genius in Covey's concepts.

14. "Open Doors" has been monitoring persecution of Christians worldwide since the seventies. The report referenced here can be found at https://www.opendoorsusa.org/christian-persecution/world-watch-list/about-wwl-ranking.
15. Per discipleallnations.com (2013 data)
16. Michael Horton's *Ordinary* is a wonderful companion to David Platt's book, *Radical*. Horton and Platt hold different views of ministry, but both offer great insight. Read both books!
17. *The Purpose Driven Church* continues to help churches around the world. I'm not sure that there has been a more impactful book for church leaders published in the past thirty years.
18. *Holy Discontent* is another must read for pastors and church leaders.
19. One of my favorite books on Martin Luther King, Jr. was written by the man himself. *The Autobiography of Martin Luther King, Jr.*, edited by Clayborne Carson, is an amazing read.
20. Beechwood was a wonderful church to serve. My family and I joined in membership in 1998, and in 2005 I began to serve the church as its Executive Director of Ministries. This church will always hold a special place in my heart! To learn more about Beechwood, go to beechwoodchurch.org.
21. The definitions given for each of the five annual planning steps come from merriam-webster.com
22. *Mere Christianity* offers so much wisdom that goodreads.com provides seven web pages filled with quotes from this classic book! (https://www.goodreads.com/work/quotes/801500-mere-christianity).
23. I had the joy and privilege of being mentored by Kevin Harney for around a year as he led a small group of church leaders through implementing *Organic Outreach*. Not only was this a time of great learning for myself, but I have seen firsthand the incredible impact of *Organic Outreach*. Learn more at http://www.organicoutreach.com.

24. I served Remembrance from 2012 until 2015, and was blessed to serve the Lord and His people there. To learn more about Remembrance, go to remembrancechurch.org.

25. *In Search of Excellence*, while published more than thirty years ago, continues to be a valuable resource for business leaders. In fact, many consider *In Search of Excellence* to be the best business book of all time.

26. Over the years I have read a lot of reports on how much to allocate for human resources in a church. Admittedly, there remains a wide variety of opinions, but in general there is consensus around a 45-55% range. However, each church is different, so if you use this range, do so as a guideline rather than as a hard and fast rule.

27. From *The Cure for the Common Life*, by Max Lucado.

28. This is one amazing church! Learn more by going to http://crosstolight.com/haiti/church-plants/cap-haitien.

29. *Money Matters in the Church* is my go-to resource for church budgeting. Malphurs and Stroope have a wealth of wisdom and experience in this area.

30. Malachi 3:10

31. Acts 2:9-11

32. 2 Timothy 4:2 NRSV

33. http://www.lifeway.com/Article/research-survey-sharing-christ-2012.

34. Dr. Rainer's research and insight are a remarkable gift to church leaders around the world.

35. From *The Genuine Works of Flavius Josephus*, by Flavius Josephus.

36. Through one-on-one mentoring relationships between adult church members and at-risk elementary school-children, Kids Hope USA works to meet the emotional, social and academic needs of children. I have been blessed to serve as a mentor for eleven years as part of the Kids Hope USA ministry in the churches I served.

37. From blueletterbible.org
38. The Vision Convergence Worksheet, while unique, was inspired by and rooted in the "Vision Intersection Profile" (VIP) in *Breakout Churches*, by Thom Rainer. I simply added a few additional elements to Rainer's VIP. *Breakout Churches* remains a ground breaking, must read book for all churches that are serious about making disciples.

MICHAEL GAFA

Michael Gafa serves the Reformed Church in America as a Classis Leader in North Grand Rapids, and as a consultant for leadership development and strengthening churches in the Region of the Great Lakes. Michael is married to Pamela, and is a proud father of twin sons Spencer and Trevor.

ADDITIONAL RESOURCES:

Web: faithbasedplanning.org
Email: faithbasedplanning@gmail.com

64497908R00166

Made in the USA
Lexington, KY
10 June 2017